50p

KT-153-195

TRAMPING SCOTTISH HILLS

R.K.H.

SGOR A MHAIM, GLEN NEVIS

TRAMPING
SCOTTISH HILLS

BY
W. KERSLEY HOLMES

*With twelve plates from photographs by
the Author and by R. K. Holmes.*

ENEAS MACKAY
STIRLING
1946

TO
NANCY AND MELVILLE

Printed at the Observer Press, 40 Craigs, Stirling, Scotland

FOREWORD

This is not a book of mountaineering exploits, nor a guide-book in any sense of the term. All it aims at is to collect some reminiscences of days on the open road and amongst the heights of Scotland where there are no roads of any kind. Countless other lovers of the hills have wider experience than mine, and more adventures in their memory, and if they would put that experience and those adventures on paper I should be an enthusiastic reader. Having written what this book contains, I hope others will enjoy comparing their impressions with mine, disagreeing with me here and there, but finding their enthusiasm heightened and their own recollections revived.

Any writer of a book which touches on mountains is faced by the problem of indicating what standards of climbing he has to consider. Some mountaineering authors mislead the average reader by assuming that he is equally at home on the rocks ; thus one speaks of the Sgur nan Gillean ridge traverse as a " walk." I do not think it fair to describe so any expedition which involves the use of the hands as well as the feet. Accepting his standard, there is hardly a " climb " described in these pages, but, for any reader whose exercise is generally taken on the level, " climbs " is the only word for such ascents as, for instance, that of Ben Lui by the Northern gully. Yet even for his sake I cannot apply the word climb to the mounting of the path up Ben Lomond, to give a popular example. Perhaps I might say that I have written of nothing more severe than scrambles. If the rope and the ice-axe appear, it is by chance, and as a kind of decoration.

The term " Munros " means Scottish tops of three thousand feet and above, as classified by the late Sir Hugh Munro.

Though no lover of hills can explain his devotion, or what reward it wins for him, he finds it pleasant to find what he, more or less inarticulate, feels in the heart's core, expressed by men whose words none can take lightly. " I think that to look at mountains for a year is an education," says Lord Dunsany. What good mountains do us I cannot say, but education goes beyond our sight. I feel that to be amongst mountains is to be taken for a while amongst very august company, they have an ancient wisdom among them which we cannot understand, but we are better for having looked upon the mere faces of those that possess it." And what says, more boldly, the mystic William Blake ?

" Great things are done when men and mountains meet;
They are not done by jostling in the street."

CONTENTS

viii CONTENTS

PLATES

CHAPTER ONE

THE OCHILS AND THEREABOUTS

IT is appropriate that this book should start from Dollar, in Clackmannanshire, Scotland's smallest county, for its neighbourhood is the area in which the writer learned to love the kind of walking which has for many a year been his chief recreation. I recommend the same simple countryside to any starter on the trail—the endless trail of those who find walking their chief outdoor entertainment.

Dollar has a famous school, Dollar Academy, founded in 1815, and named also " John MacNabb's School " after the local shepherd boy who made a fortune in London, and left it for the good of the Parish.

Lucky the boys and girls educated there, in the midst of quiet beauty, with the grassy Ochils as an extra, unrestricted playground. Their highest point, Ben Cleuch, attains no greater dignity than the modest height of 2,363 feet, but hills do not depend on altitude for their interest. The range is extensive enough to afford, with the variations of season and weather, ample scope for hard exercise and for apprenticeship to some of the essentials of mountain lore and craft. By mountain craft I am not thinking of the gymnastic skill of the cragsman, but of the ability to find the way in any circumstances ; to appreciate situations as regards weather, to plan according to your powers, and so forth.

A couple of centuries ago a forgotten and very

minor poet, James Kennedy by name, referring to
the Ochils' highest point, wrote that

" Proud Bencloch parts the ambient air,
A beauteous cone, remotely seen,
Commanding many a belvedere."

What he had in mind as belvederes I do not know,
but it certainly is locally claimed for Ben Cleuch—as
for so many points of vantage—that it commands
" the finest view in Scotland." Such superlatives are
contentious ; let it suffice to say that Ben Cleuch, like
its slightly lower neighbours, King's Seat and White
Wisp, dominates a really wonderful panorama on a
clear day. From one or other of those tops you may
see the Forth and the Tay Bridges ; Tinto Hill in
Lanarkshire ; the Bass Rock, the Pentlands, a great
frieze of mountain silhouettes from Ben Lomond to the
Cairngorms, and under specially favourable conditions,
Ben Nevis, sixty miles away.

(A particular pleasure is theirs who can not only
identify distant heights, but who can also greet them as
acquaintances. What a chapter of retrospect, then,
when you have climbed plenty of the Scottish Hills, to
return to any one of them and contemplate the others !
I hope the reader is of the kind who can enter into this
sentiment).

Naturally, nearer than these landmarks, lies a
great stretch of varied country, mostly agricultural ;
through the middle distance meanders the silver-
shining Forth ; and the keen eye may pick out ships
lying at Rosyth, and beyond them the spires and towers
of Edinburgh.

To those familiar with the Ochils and similar almost

" domesticated " ranges, from their childhood, it seems strange to find others who have lived for years almost on their flanks and who have felt, but never yielded to, the longing to walk amongst them.

They may be heard to say that they have never gone because there was nobody to " take " them. Almost as perplexing to the lucky country-bred are those who ask, hopefully, if there are paths to the points they aspire to reach.

If any reader of these pages is amongst those thus handicapped by lack of confidence, and by the obsession of the beaten track, let him break the spell by experiment, aided by a map and a compass and controlled by commonsense. The experienced are self-reliant, but they had to gain their experience.

First experiments should be modest. Tramping up hill and down on rough ground makes a sterner demand on the wind and the muscles than walking on the flat ; excessive ambition, contempt for even those grassy slopes, may tempt to trial trips which end in aches, blisters and disgust.

Perhaps this is as good an opportunity as any for a word or two about solitary hill-tramping. The very cautious advise against it unconditionally ; the reasonable say it is foolish if conditions are tough. Leaving altogether out of the question solitary crag-climbing, climbing proper, it is certainly true that anywhere—and even on the most amiable summer day—you might sprain an ankle badly and find difficulty enough in reaching help. In bad weather you might lose your way and be completely exhausted before finding it again. Yet those mischances very rarely happen ; perhaps when you are alone you use, unconsciously, a fraction more care than when you have company. It is only right to bear in mind that if evil does befall you, and you fail to get home, you are going to give others a great deal of trouble. To minimise this hypothetical bother you can make it a rule, as far as possible to indicate roughly whither you are bound, so that the search-party will have some idea where to look for the body.

Against the quite sensible arguments in favour of company may be mentioned the fact that even expert mountain-climbers—who add their voices to the chorus of caution—frequently go alone. Read their books and see. They understand something which it seems only the hill-lover knows—that while days on the tops with the right friends can be as nearly perfect as any days of human life, an occasional expedition by yourself makes you free of the mountain-mystery in a very special way. You are certainly more sensitive to every sort of impression, with no distractions outside your own head. An elderly lady once told me that her friends, perplexed by her liking for an occasional country ramble without company, asked if she didn't want someone to talk to: " I like to listen to myself sometimes," was her answer. Loneliness in the heart of the hills—hills wide in expanse like the Cairngorms, or hills far more humble transformed by darkness or mist—can be eerie in the extreme. To discover this, and thereby to learn something unsuspected about yourself, is in itself an experience worth having. And from the practical point of view, you will progress in your hill-craft far more rapidly when you have only yourself to rely upon than when you have a friend to consult.

The hill-walker starting his career even on such easy slopes as the Ochils might as well enjoy the comfort and convenience of suitable equipment. Experience has taught me to wear sturdy boots, not shoes. Shoes I have found apt to lead to blisters, and grit gets into them. Boots may save you a twisted ankle. Your walking will be greatly aided by some goodly nails in your footgear—not only on the sole and heel, but under the arch of the instep also. It was a Cruachan shepherd who recommended those to me, pointing out how often they may save a slip on a rock hidden by heather or in a jungle of bracken.

To carry an extra garment, if only a muffler, is sensible, for even in summer you may find a keen wind on the tops, and it is pleasant to be able to coddle yourself a little when you sit for lunch beside your captured cairn. In winter let your spare apparel be too much rather than too little. What a miserable specimen I have repeatedly found myself as penalty for disregarding the voice of commonsense on this matter! Get accustomed to a rucksack—not necessarily one of those which look as if they could contain all a man's moveables—and you will find it an admirable companion if stocked with the right odds and ends, such as more grub than you expect to want, and some decent string in case a bootlace, or your braces, or anything else replaceable by string, gives way.

Let me here say a few words about the rucksack, even if they amount to a confession. I have never gone " bowed beneath a weight like that we sometimes feel in dreams," even for the sake of being able to camp and cook en route. I like country and I like good meals, but to carry on my back while I walk and scramble the essentials for camping and cooking would just spoil the objects of my outings, which are primarily walking and scrambling. As a result of doing Schiehallion with a heavier pack than usual I got a wrong impression of that mountain ; it figured in my mind as one of the " sulky " hills till I made a second pilgrimage without an unforgettable burden.

I remember tramping with a Canadian " exploraatory surveyor," on holiday in Scotland from sub-arctic British Columbia ; we saw a good many hikers—around Arrochar this was—and his comment was that he and his crew would never dream of tackling distances beneath such weights, or in boots with such vast protruding steel-fanged welts !

For winter hill-walking a balaclava is the thing. When you find hail or sleet, or even a really toothy wind, attacking you from a flank, you will be very glad to pull it down over your ears. Gloves are of course essential ; they are desirable on many days of the milder seasons, if you are chilly-fingered by constitution.

In winter never—or hardly ever—go any distance without a compass. Even if you don't need it you may practise the use of it for the emergency when you do. Perhaps this sounds absurd, particularly when referring to such sheep-pastures as the Ochils, but a compass can at least help you sometimes to reach your objective more quickly than if you were left to instinct. You can always " get somewhere," of course, by following down a burn, but it may be into the wrong valley. I speak as one whose sense of direction cannot be first rate—one who has trudged an hour's circle through mist and made the humiliating discovery of his own spoor in the snow to prove that the figure was completed.

R.K.H.

GLENDEVON, IN THE OCHILS

To come back from generalizations to the Ochils ; when I refer to them as sheep-pastures I am being hardly fair. Even towards the eastern end of the range, where they subside and smoothen towards their vanishing-point, steep braes can be found ; and at the western end stand such buttresses as Craigleith and Dumyat, with rocky fronts that are a challenge to the cragsman, but which I do not recommend to him, the rock being treacherous, tending to " come away in your hand." And it is worth remarking that a very smooth, steep grass-slope can be really dangerous in summer, if, as in some of the Ochil glens, they terminate in cliffs above a burn. Grass can become well-nigh as slippery as ice ; have some of us not tobogganed on it under an August sun ?

You may choose from a variety of ways to get to the top of Bencleuch. The steepest and most direct is from Tillicoultry, and that route starts up Tillicoultry Glen, which is well worth seeing for its own sake— quite a wild gorge towards its upper end. The way from Dollar is longer but gentler. Perhaps the most usual way is to follow up various burns which the map will show you, but my favourite route, and the sort of route I recommend, is over the intervening heights of King's Seat and Gannel Hill—which, on some maps, is oddly named Andrew Gannel, though nobody seems to know who the gentleman was. (After all, there is a hill called " Robinson " in the English Lake District, and mountains in Skye whose names are the Gaelic version of the names of individuals worthy of such noble memorials). That makes a switch-back walk, but surely it is more enjoyable to be on high ground all the time, with wide views around and dry going ? The

B

craze for following up burns is an obsession with people who don't go much about hills. It can be terribly fatiguing, involving many little detours, the negotiation of tributaries, and the dodging of countless bogs, and in summer, persecution by the bloodthirsty insect legions.

How long should you take, there and back ? How should such a question be best answered ? The double journey has been done, from Dollar, in two hours. But then a hundred yards has been run in under ten seconds ! You may not be out for athletics. Six hours would be reasonable, but on a perfect day surely you should forget the clock. You might go up from Dollar and descend into Tillicoultry, completing the round by 'bus or train, unless you are one of the many who feel, after long hours on the hill, that the steady rhythm of a mile or two on the flat is the most satisfactory finish. It used to be quite a fashion amongst enthusiasts to climb Ben Cleuch in time to watch the sunrise. Such expeditions are bound to be hit or miss ventures, but the lucky occasion compensates for many disappointments. Perhaps my own finest reward was a sight of what is called the Green Ray. Jules Verne wrote an amusing book about it, telling the adventures of a party who made an expedition to the Hebrides, intent on seeing the sun rise from a sea horizon, with the chance of the thrill of that special phenomenon. They—like the author—obviously supposed that the green ray is seen only with that condition, but they were wrong. Lord Dunsany in *While the Syrens Slept* tells that it is a common spectacle in the desert, and when the sun rose for me with one swift flash of flaming emerald it certainly ascended over a land horizon. That colour endured for only the fraction of a second; the next moment it was replaced by white incandescence intolerable to the eye.

The morning spectacle apart, the trudge up any hill on a summer night is an experience worth gaining. The coolness of the air after a glowing day is exhilarating, and the scent of the wet grass and bracken under your tread is one of those which haunts you. " Smells are surer than sounds or sights " as an evocation ! Alone, you can indulge any fancy you like, bred of the night with its voices—some of the voices of day magnified, as the tiny burns whisper and chatter, and a roused bird rises, and any moving breath of air is an audible sigh amongst the dew-hung grass. Uncanny ? Yes ; you remember many an old story ; absurd superstitions begin to seem not quite so indefensible.

This sunrise-attending is usually a bleak business, however rewarding. Just before dawn a bitter little draught seems to blow along the hills, a shivery breath ; it stirs the ocean of mist in the valleys ; those grey, stationary " billows " of it, which have lain for hours against the dark surmounting peaks, move and thin and disperse. Sometimes the whole surface of the mist begins to flow, so that from the heights you seem to be looking down on to a wide, swift, silent current.

After the sun has risen clear above the horizon you are not disposed to linger. The show, successful or disappointing, is over ; the next thing is to get warm as soon as possible, and home. Luckily, going downhill quickly rids your bones of the shivers, and within half an hour you may well find it difficult to recall the sensation of being really cold.

I have said a good deal about Ben Cleuch, as one

is apt to do about the highest of any range, but all over the Ochils there is grand, easy tramping country. Perhaps the most popular of all walks there is that through Glen Quey to Glendevon, where you may have a meal. My recommendation is that some day you continue the pilgrimage to Auchterarder, whither, from Glendevon, runs an ancient grass-covered track delightful for the feet. For the first two miles it winds upwards along the side of green slopes, a kind of terrace, and from the summit offers a view which has startled many with its sudden panorama of northern mountains. The whole walk—despite the last rather dull mile or so into Auchterarder itself—calls for lyrical treatment. The area through which it goes always figures in my mind as " The Kingdom of the Whaups," for on a lucky spring day the call of those birds dominates everything, seconded by the voices of lambs and the interwoven songs of countless larks, making a music which seems one with the blue of the sky and the gold of the sunshine.

It would be ridiculous to discuss the neighbourhood of Dollar as a walker's paradise and to make no mention of Castle Campbell, a noble old keep magnificently situated on a knoll high above the valley. To reach it you have a choice of ways, the best, really sensational, being through the glen, which has been described as the most remarkable gorge in Scotland. It is certainly impressive, but unfortunately the finest, most awesome stretch of it has been for some years out of commission, owing to falls of rock and trees, and the breaking of bridges which could not in wartime be repaired. You can however approach the old building —where Mary Queen of Scots did really once spend a night !—by a rough road past the quarry on the adjacent Gloom Hill. Perhaps by the time you read this it will be possible once more as in the past to have tea in the caretaker's quarters in the castle ; if not, you can walk round outside and see what an impressive landmark the place is from any point of view. The taking over, in 1946, of the Castle and Glen by the National Trust for Scotland, ensured that both would be preserved for future generations.

One of the most remarkable features of Castle Campbell Glen is Kemp's Score, a steep narrow gash from the top of the Castle crag right down to the burn that forces its troubled way through the dark " canyon " below. If you walk round the castle to the green knoll south of the building you can look down the Score, which descends close to a detached old archway of fine solid masonry. Sir Walter Scott records in his Journal that, revisiting the place in his maturity, he took that look down, and was astonished to remember that as a young man he had not been contented to gaze, but had also climbed. He speaks as if it were a really terrible place to tackle; frankly, it isn't. It has often and often been done by schoolboys and others, both ways. Getting thoroughly muddy is the worst that is likely to happen to you.

Visible on the lower slopes of White Wisp, which looks down on Castle Campbell from the north-east, is the gable of a ruined house, Craiginnan Farm. This has a special interest as once the dwelling of one John Christie, born early in the 18th century, who lived there with two sisters and owned some three hundred and seventy books—a considerable library for a man of his station in those days. I hear youngsters now refer to the place as " Library Farm," and am rather pleased.

One of Dollar's most popular walks is—or was—known as the Five Mile Round. It takes you twice across the Devon, at one point by a modern concrete bridge of which perhaps the less said the better, at the other by a single old stone arch upon which you are bound to linger. That is " Vicar's Bridge ", and commemorates a vicar who, according to a lettered stone outside the parapet, "among other acts of benevolence built this bridge and died a martyr in 1538." Thomas Forret, or Forrest, was at one time Canon of Inchcolm. Too advanced for his time, he was sent to Dollar, but despite warnings, he continued to read the Bible to his congregation in English, and in other ways to show Lutheran tendencies. He was burned at Edinburgh. The present bridge appears to be a widening of the old. The best way to check this assertion is to float underneath it on your back, but you are warned that the stream here is deep and never warm.

Not far up the hill from Vicar's Bridge to Blairingone is an oak-tree on the left hand side of the road, bearing in its bark the nearly obscured initials " J.B." and a cross. That tree has a history, for behind it, one night early in the last century, lay Joe Bell with a gun, in ambush for a baker. This old crime is interesting chiefly because Bell, who was executed at Perth, was the last man to be hanged publicly in Scotland ; tradition says that a local worthy, by way of honeymoon, took his bride to Perth for the occasion.

Years ago, I remember, it was said that the neighbourhood was haunted ; that you could hear the wheels of a ghostly baker's ghostly cart on the rough road—laden, presumably, with the ghosts of bannocks and cookies. Though you will be disappointed if you expect that particular thrill, you will find Vicar's Bridge a slightly uneasy spot for lingering, alone, at night. Woods used to surround it, and the gloom conspired against your nerves with the gurgle of the black eddies below the arch and perhaps the demoniac screech of a hunting owl. Since many of the trees have been felled, the place has lost some, but not all, of its special " atmosphere." You will prefer it on a blazing summer day, when you may picnic on the shingle above the bridge and watch the sun-dazzle on the rapids, and the glint of innumerable insects in the beams, and when the voice from the woods is that of the wood-pigeon or the pheasant.

Four miles above Dollar there is another notable bridge, a double one ; it is known as Rumbling Bridge, and if you lean over the parapet and look down you will find your gaze plunging into a really remarkable water-worn gorge. Why " Rumbling " Bridge ? Stroll about the paths in the hotel grounds, till you find yourself near the water's edge, and your ears will explain. In a spate, particularly, the rumble is awesome ; listen and you will hear the " Devil's Mill " at work—the angry water growling and pounding in the cauldron-prisons it has ground for itself in the course of ages.

A mile down the river from Rumbling Bridge— where there is a railway station, by the way—is another feature of the Devon ; one which seems nowadays to be seldom visited, and yet which would, in some districts, be considered a " sight " worth publicising. It is one of the most striking pieces of river scenery that I know, this waterfall known as the Cauldron Linn. It owes its existence, geologists tell me, to the presence amongst softer rock of a ledge of dolerite. This forms one side of an amphitheatre some eighty feet high, the river plunging into the bottom of it through a narrow opening that produces strange effects when the river is coming down in style. An unremitting toiler with untold centuries for its task, the stream has formed two dark, smooth-sided cauldrons, and now plunges from one to the other before making the final leap which lands it crashing on to a great pile of rocks fallen from the crags above. The paths around it are disappearing, but at the expense of a scramble you must see this fall both from above and below—trying to disregard the dreadful eyesore of certain piping which runs along the cliff at one side, conveying water for power to a house not far away. From above you can watch the sudden hurry and plunge of the compressed current and the rainbows in the rising spray, and listen to the jackdaws that inhabit the ivied cliffs ; from below you can well-nigh hypnotise yourself by concentrating on the hurtling white water in its sombre setting. At dusk, if the river is really big, and the water is coming over in masses that sometimes rebound in geyser-spouts as high as the cliff-tops, and the whole gorge is smoking with spray and vapour, there are voices in the Cauldron Linn that can hold you listening till you feel that you are an intruder amongst powers too ancient and too great to tolerate your presence indefinitely. Perhaps this is true of all big waterfalls ; I am speaking for this one.

Before turning my back on Dollar and the Ochils I must recommend one more expedition ; the walk through the hills to the little village of Blackford, which has a station on the main Perth line. Before

setting out you had better study the map carefully,
or you may be misled by burns, and descend in quite
the wrong place. My favourite route has always been
over the hill King's Seat (2111 feet) and down its
north-western side to strike a very old path which brings
you—if scrupulously followed despite its efforts at con-
cealment here and there—first to a lonely cottage,
Back Hill House, the home of a shepherd, and thence
right up little Glen Bee and down into Blackford. On
a fine bright day there is nothing in this but a straight-
forward nine-mile, fairly rough walk, but if you like to
test your powers more severely, try it in midwinter, and
you may acquire considerable respect for these Ochils.
Many a year ago two men died in the snow somewhere
on that path—or so tradition says. It has a strong
personal interest for me because for more than twenty
years it was a New Year pilgrim route for a few of us,
the regulation being that we went whether the weather
permitted or not. We have had some toughish times,
for rain or sleet, driven before a stiff wind, can be an
ungentle adversary on some of the more open stretches ;
and if there is deep soft snow, or sleet, poor condition
is found out all right. Sometimes, reaching our
favourite place of refreshment at Blackford, we have
had to take off and empty our boots as a preliminary
to the ham-and-eggs and tea that made all the discomfort worth while. On the other hand, we have arrived
scorched with the sunshine reflected from hard snow,
or armoured with clinging sleet that melted as we ate—
barefooted, with our socks in the fender.

The New Year ritual involved walking back to
Dollar, through Gleneagles. A main road runs through
that long cleft on the eastern side, but on the left is a

far more interesting grassy track, warmly to be recommended if there is light enough by that time.   It is a
lovely place on a spring or summer day, and a strange,
hushed, half-haunted one after dusk when perhaps a
the moon is rising over the abrupt slopes opposite. You
won't much enjoy the last ten or so miles on the hard
high road unless you are one of those who enjoy a
steady left, right, for an hour or two, after a long spell
of picking steps on rough country, but the trudge makes
a satisfactory finish to a round which measures a mile
or two over the twenty.   And you have the chance of
sitting down and reinforcing your powers at Glendevon.
The whole of this book might be taken up with the
subject of walks round Dollar.   For instance, a tramp
across the valley from the Cleish direction is one to
include in any active holiday plan.   You might be
transported, to give you a good start, to the little
Village of Powmill, south of Rumbling Bridge, and
thence mount on to the Cleish Hills, going via Cult Hill
to Weather Hill (1,100 ft.), and on to Dunglow (1,241 ft.).
Turning north, aim for Seamab Hill above Muckhart,
taking every by-way that presents itself, and all the
way you will enjoy an aspect of the Ochils, and the
lovely vista of the valley with Stirling Castle and the
Wallace Monument against the western sky, and
instead of walking tamely by the highroad back to
Dollar, climb your landmark, Seamab (1,442 ft.), and
make your way home along the grassy front of the
Ochils.   This is a walk for those " in trim."

CHAPTER TWO

THE LOMONDS

KINROSS-SHIRE may not occur to you as a county in which to look for the kind of walking with which this book is concerned, and yet a visit with your hill-boots will have its rewards. The Lomond Hills rise nowhere to more than 1,800 feet, but they have their characteristics and some extremely interesting details—for which a certain amount of geological mixture is to be thanked.

Kinross-shire, for so many, means Loch Leven, famous for the imprisonment and romantic escape of Mary Queen of Scots, but still more renowned for its trout. The loch is not really a picturesque sheet of water, largely because of the flatness of the country immediately surrounding it. Benarty Hill on the south and the grassy Lomonds on the east do their best to supply pleasant backgrounds, but I do not think many of those who go round it in cars have any idea what they might discover if they lingered here and there. How many of them have stopped and really explored the charming little village of Kinnesswood, for example ? Yet it is one of the prettiest villages I know in Scotland. It has climbing, winding, cobbled causeys to lead to old houses and cottages, with rich-hued tiled roofs and crow-stepped gables, set with charming lack of plan amongst their sun-trap gardens.

One of those old buildings is maintained as a humble " museum " where the exhibits are associated with Michael Bruce, the poet of the *Ode to the Skylark*, a native of the place, or with his times.

If you happen to be anything of an artist, either with brush or camera, Kinnesswood will delay you ; but sooner or later tear yourself away and mount the braes above the village. You may with luck see a fox or two at his ease in some glade amongst the bracken which coats the lower slopes.

Two particular spots may serve as objectives for short walks. One is the line of crags which make a bastion along the northern face of Bishop Hill and White Craigs ; the particular detail to look for there is a remarkable rock pinnacle known as Carlin Maggie. It consists of a series of boulders one on the top of another—doubtless the remains of eroded strata—the smallest being, at a rough estimate, forty feet from the base. It is all the more impressive from its situation ; seen from behind, it stands up like a spire with the sunlit valley well below, and the gentle outlines of the Ochils for a background.

Another pretext for a Lomond ramble from Kinnesswood is a little gorge called Glenvale—a surprising sort of feature to find hereabouts. A path, skirting the north-eastern slopes, will guide you to Glenvale. It is only a grassy cleft cut by the pretty burn that runs down it, but at its head there is a water-fall, with a " Pulpit Rock " and other picturesque masses around it. They are, I think, a kind of sandstone, and have been water or weather-worn in a very curious way.

Glenvale on a warm summer day would be an ideal picnic-place. Elsewhere on the Lomonds there are other rock-curiosities. One such is a mass resemb-

ling a huge toadstool, the great circular top being
supported by a circular stalk.   This is another
example of the freakish sculpture which, in the course
of ages, the patient unresting powers of wind and frost
and rain collaborate to produce.   It will be found by
the explorer on the lower slopes of West Lomond.

CHAPTER THREE

BEN VENUE

BEN Venue is in every way a most beautiful mountain; in a sense, it seems to me to be a kind of epitome of the Scottish Highlands. The tourist from England or abroad is too often shewn the Trossachs and Loch Lomond as sample show-pieces; having seen them, from car, 'bus, or steamer, he is allowed to have the impression that he knows what the Scottish Highlands are like. If, into the bargain, he were coaxed or encouraged to climb Ben Venue, he would realise some of the characteristics of Caledonia which, without that experience, remain unknown to him.

Of course it is impossible to think of Ben Venue without the appearance in the mind of tags from *The Lady of the Lake*, a poem which, whether it is now read or not, has in a most remarkable way captured the " atmosphere " of the stretch of glorious country in which its scene is laid. Since Scott's time his genial spirit haunts the crags and glens and shaggy woods all around Loch Katrine; the landscape and the poet are mutually indebted.

Venue is magnificently situated, and its formation is worthy of its setting. It is not amongst the mountain aristocrats as regards height, but what it lacks in elevation—it is only 2,393 feet—it more than makes up in ruggedness and beauty.

My usual approach is from Aberfoyle. I take the road known as " The Duke's Road " or " The Toll Road," which climbs very steeply out of " the clachan

of Aberfoyle " at the west end and crosses over the hill
to the Trossachs. I quit that road and take to the
brae just past the quarries. (I remember that road
when it was a mere track, not open to wheeled traffic.
The views it offers are as wonderful as ever, but it
cannot be quite the ideal " hiker's way " of my first
acquaintance).

The run of the contours on your map indicates
that Venue is easiest ascended from the quarries by a
wide ridge running west, then curving round from north
to east. Follow the crest of that formation, and you
will achieve the rugged double top without difficulty—
but not without some rough going. Its general rich
ruggedness is one of the charms of Ben Venue. Its
height is only thirty feet above that of my dear old friend
Ben Cleuch—but what a difference in character from
that green mound! The rockiness of the crests of Ben
Venue will delight you if you appreciate the pictures
that can be made by crags and heather in a fine free
jumble.

It was my luck to be up there once when circumstances produced what might be regarded as the perfect
Highland picture. Alternate showers and sunshine
gave brilliance to every colour ; then a rainbow formed,
and under its arch, or so it seemed, paced a herd of deer
at their easy graceful leisure, for I was too far away to
be noticed.

Should you want a scramble, descend by the face
that frowns in splendid dignity down on to the Trossachs.
It is steep and broken, and even demands a certain
amount of caution, but it is a very much quicker descent
than that by the way you came.

Do not omit Ben Venue from your plans when you

are projecting a pilgrimage amongst Scottish hills.   It is a gem amongst mountains—a gem, glorious in its roughness.

CHAPTER FOUR

BEN LEDI

QUEEN VICTORIA, it is recorded, reached the top of Ben Ledi on pony-back, which indicates that it is not a hill that need test the powers of any two-legged walker. The route her mount followed was from the vicinity of Coilantogle on Loch Vennachar. After about three miles easy ascent, interrupted by only one short steepish stretch, where Her Majesty may have dismounted and walked, it brings you to the handsome cairn.

From Callander Ben Ledi has the appearance of a peak ; it is in fact a ridge, with crags on its eastern face. Amongst those crags are some gullies, easy enough, but certainly prohibitive to ponies, and if you want an outing more interesting than a simple walk up a grass slope, I suggest that you pick one of those as your way.

Start up the road through the Pass of Leny, cross the river by the bridge about a mile above the falls, and then, from somewhere about the farm of Coire-chrombie, make up the broken, rock-scattered slopes and pick whichever of the gullies takes your fancy. They are filled with a mixture of rock, scree, earth, and vegetation, and you will probably have to use your hands more or less, but you will be all the better pleased with yourself when you reach the top and enjoy a fine prospect of the " Lady of the Lake " country.

Ben Ledi is only 2,873 feet in height, but it has a nobility of its own, and the steep, broken slopes by which

C

it drops down towards the railway have often seemed to me, caught in glances from a train, as finely typical of the Scottish Highlands.

Great masses of shattered rock, heather, bracken, birch, and oak-trees, torn water-courses—what colour, what light and shade effects, whether illuminated by sunshine or half-veiled and mysterious in drifting cloud-wreaths !

The derivation of names is generally disputable, but let us accept the theory, a likely one enough, that " Ledi " is somehow associated with prehistoric religious rites and ceremonial fires. That association obtruded itself on my thoughts one night when I waited there for the sunrise, that and a grim legend with death dominating it—a legend which at the time I believed to be associated with the immediate vicinity, but which really belongs elsewhere. The day had been a blazer in July—and was followed by another—but a cold east wind got up after dark, and ragged masses of cloud blew low overhead. I had an odd feeling of being an unwelcome guest of the mountain-top. Things moved in the gloom, and rustled ; mostly sheep, of course, and when I suddenly lit a cigarette they bounded off with the sheep's own alarm-whistle. The wind was strong and bitter, and I was glad to huddle in the lee of rocks which still retained a kindly hint of the evening's warmth.

Altogether it was an eerie night, as eerie as any I have spent out of doors, and I was glad when the darkness began to thin and I could pick my way carefully in the direction of Ben Vane, about four miles northwards.

The sunrise was something of a disappointment,

without any splendours ; the sky merely got brighter and brighter until here was full daylight, with still air and every promise of the grand morning and afternoon of gold and blue that followed.

I sat contentedly on the hillside above Strathyre until the chimneys had begun to send up their blue wisps, and then made my way down to the village, more contentedly still, for it was the way to breakfast.

When Ben Ledi is mentioned, I always remember that vigil of mine ; I also remember being told by an elderly gentleman that one very early morning in his youth he had arrived at the summit, like me to see the sunrise, and there met another enthusiast—in a night-gown. The explanation was that, finding himself extremely cold, he had donned every garment in his knapsack, with the nightshirt, as roomiest, over the lot. This was before the days of pyjamas ; pyjamas, falling short of the nightshirt in incongruity, would not have produced quite so memorable a picture.

A third incident is associated for me with Ben Ledi. A policeman once told me that in his younger days he and a chum used to bring in every New Year on the summit. They had a tiny tent, and were very snug, particularly when there was snow to bank around it. One year they thought they would have a hike on the level instead, and evening found them on the side of Loch Earn. It was a dirty night, wet and black, and at length they decided they would bivouac on the first patch of grass they could discover. Presently they found a patch—quite by the sense of touch ; got up their tent somehow, and slept.

When dawn came, they broke camp in an unusual hurry, for they found themselves on the lawn under the windows of St. Fillans hotel !

CHAPTER FIVE

BEN LOMOND

EVERYBODY'S hill? Glasgow's mountain? Sometimes those to whom it is a familiar landmark—and the peak is visible from points within the city boundary—think of Ben Lomond a little patronizingly, as though it were a feature of their own back garden. Yet, amongst those who really know hills, only the snob could belittle "the Ben." I prefer the attitude of those Glasgow people who, though they may never have climbed it, seem to regard it as an object of personal pride. One very clear day I had an argument with an elderly representative of this attitude, and made him almost angry by maintaining that a certain top visible from the flagstaff in Queen's Park, and showing just west of Dumgoyne, was not his beloved Ben but Stobinian occulting Ben More. Knowing I was right—for the tip of Ben Lomond was below the level of the Kilpatrick hills—I could not pretend that he had persuaded me, and I fear I left him still to gaze at that faint blue pyramid as his beloved Ben Lomond. I feel a little doubt whether he knew the name of any other hill it might be.

The usual way up Ben Lomond is from Rowardennan, where a sign indicates the start of the four miles of path. It is an easy path, but before you reach the summit, at 3,192 feet, you may think it physically wearisome enough unless you are accustomed to walking up slopes of that length. The lower part is usually wet, but if you are anything of a botanist you will find some compensation for that in the presence, in their season, of various little hill-plants which love a marshy habitat ; typical are the insectivorous sundew and the butter-wort, the latter conspicuous by its dark purple-blue flower gracefully hung on the tall stem which rises from the centre of a star of leaves lying flat on the ground.

The track makes a wide circuit to avoid the glen cutting the front of the hill, and under certain conditions it is possible to wander from it, particularly as it passes across a stretch of fairly level drier ground where it is never as plain as in its other sections.

Another and more obvious consolation is the view, more and more wonderful with every hundred feet of height that is gained. Those who have never seen the Loch and its islands from the shoulder of the Ben have never seen it properly at all.

The right way to learn to love Ben Lomond is to pick a settled fine day and permit no consideration to hurry you. All your life afterwards you will remember that experience, particularly if you are not a habitual hill-climber, as a kind of revelation. To give a foreign visitor an idea of what is connoted by the term " the Scottish Highlands " I would far rather take him up Ben Lomond or, as I have said earlier, Ben Venue— and make him constantly turn to admire the prospect, than transport him through the Trossachs. I should encourage him to bask on the summit, perhaps to have a dip, if he felt warm on the descent, in a certain pool which has served as tub for me.

Later, for the increasing of his familiarity with the country he is sure to have heard described as stern and wild, I should lure him into an ascent on one of those days when the grey clouds are clinging and trailing along the sombre slopes a couple of hundred feet above the dark, rain-blurred loch. In such weather the hope of keeping dry is soon exorcised and you splash on unconcerned, though for a good deal of the way you might as well be tramping up the bed of a burn.

He might well ask, before we set forth, what was the use of wading and labouring up three thousand feet when visibility from the top must be next to nil ; if on our return he considered that our efforts had been wasted I should know that he was no mountaineer—no real out-of-door man at all, in fact. A wide view from a hill-top is a treat indeed, but it is not for the distant view that I and others like me climb hills ; we regard those views as a bonus.

Why do we climb, then ? The question should not be asked, for all the answers it is possible to formulate miss the mark. We don't really know, but I might mention amongst the rewards that sense of being high up, the great silence and the hours spent amongst nature's wonders and beauties, which changes of weather do but vary.

On such a day as I have suggested for my visitor's second Ben Lomond expedition he might not see anything more than a hundred yards away, but he would have a chance of being impressed by the beauty of the moving mist around him, veils enclosing him as he advanced ; and of appreciating the marvels of beauty around him and under his feet—pebbles turned by wet into shining jewels, tiny plants and glowing mosses, even the raindrops pendant on every blade of grass.

My usual luck gave me such a day for my first ascent of Ben Lomond many a year ago. Inexperienced, I strayed off the track at the bend I have mentioned, and reached some knob which may have been the top of the spur known as the Ptarmigan. From there I took a long cast back across the soaking front of the mountain, found the path again and reached the the summit. Not unnaturally, I had that and the whole hill to myself. I felt slightly lonely and extremely insignificant when I found myself on the path that runs along the summit ridge, and looked over the other side. The hill drops sharply there in a line of crags, and under those conditions they seemed to fade into an abyss that might have been fathomless, the edge of the world. A certain guide-book which speaks of a precipice of " not less than a thousand feet " must be regarded as to some extent a work of imagination. I suppose the crags may have a sheer front of a tenth of that, and the ground drops very abruptly below them. The top of Ben Lomond, if an ideal picnic-spot on a still, radiant day, can be awesome when the clouds are down, or, again, when snow makes an altogether different mountain of it.

An alternative descent is to Inversnaid, but the inexperienced will find it long and hard going.

A most interesting alternative route for the ascent is by the east side ; steeper, drier, and more direct, but involving a good long walk before the start of the climb is reached. About halfway between Aberfoyle and Stronachlachar is a little house marked on the map as " Teapot," for the obvious and satisfactory reason. Nearly opposite the Teapot is the start of a rough but most entertaining path that curves round into Glen Dubh, down which runs the slow, dark Duchray Water to become the Forth. That track—notice some fine examples of ice-worn rocks along its route—brings you after some five miles of walking to the lonely little farm of Comer, tucked right under the slopes which you have come to mount. The desirable shoulder to climb is obvious ; it runs up steeply to bend round the cliffs which you skirt all the way to the summit.

Glen Dubh—the Dark Glen—can well deserve its appellation under certain weather conditions. One wild April day I walked up it after a tramp from Aberfoyle through flying hail, rain-showers, and bleak sunshine, and thought I had seldom seen a more inhospitable-looking mountain valley. The Ben was nearly black, with a menacing, close knot of sombre cloud about the peak. As I went ahead, the cloud-mass suddenly expressed itself in a peal of thunder, a crack short as the report of a gun, and so sudden that I jumped. After that the cloud dispersed, and I thought the mood of the day might change. Perhaps the spells of sunshine were longer, but the wind remained tempestuous and a snow-squall which coincided with my arrival at the top provided a bitterly cold welcome. Yet on a summer afternoon of heat-haze that same Glen Dubh can seem a haunt of ancient peace indeed, brimming with drowsy golden air, while the river winds along the flats as if it were too lazy to care for travelling at all. Thinking of that level stretch, I am reminded how one such day a pair of us thought we would make a small short cut by leaving the path and taking a line nearer the brink of the stream. After a few minutes' walking we wished we had not, for we found ourselves on ground that gave and swayed under our weight, as if the surface might suddenly let us through. Perhaps we should only have got wet and muddy if it had, but we were relieved to reach firmer footing, and I do not recommend anybody to follow our example.

Perhaps my brightest impression of Glen Dubh and that side of the Ben was gained very early one late spring morning, after a night spent walking from Callander. I remember noting men with bicycles and fishing-rods asleep by the roadside somewhere about the Trossachs; the gloom of the "Duke's Road" about 2 a.m. and the fright I got when I almost trod on a human form lying in the middle of it, sleeping too, though on an oddly-chosen couch ; sitting in the low crook of an old tree in Aberfoyle, wondering whether a little shower should make me modify my programme, but luckily yielding to the lure of the Ben, slowly growing clearer in the west. It was rather dark about the head of Loch Ard, and match-light was insufficient to let me read my map, and instead of going on to the Teapot I turned and fumbled my way into Glen Dubh through a rugged tangly area I should like to explore in full daylight, to check my impression that it was criss-crossed with the remains of ancient, deep worn tracks—a strange bit of country it seemed to a weary man in the dawn. Then the birds began, and I do not remember ever to have heard such an outbreak of song—I almost call it a clamour ; the place seemed crowded with birds, each voicing its ecstasy to the limits of its power.

All threats of rain had long since vanished, and Glen Dubh was a sun-trap under a deep blue sky, with every boulder on the Ben flood-lit as I waded across the stream, aiming at a shorter route than that by Comer.

I did not reach the top of the Ben on that occasion, discovering, when at length I struck the path high on the shoulder, that I was really dead beat. Perhaps had I not been half asleep my will would have made me carry on ; as it was, I turned and trudged down to the hotel at Rowardennan. There I had a trifling experience which seems worth mentioning. Flopping into a chair, I ordered tea, feeling too exhausted to think of food. On the table was a dish of marmalade, with its gold tinting the sunbeam that passed through it on to the white cloth ; in any circumstances I find that a beautiful still-life subject ; on this occasion it roused me to take and swallow a spoonful of marmalade unaccompanied ; and—it seemed to me as a result—I was at once toned up to order and make away with a large helping of ham-and-eggs and copious et ceteras, and after breakfast to take the ferry and tramp on to Alexandria.

One of Ben Lomond's special interests for me is that it is the nearest hill to Glasgow on which I have seen the ptarmigan, that lovely bird. I hope other frequenters of mountains feel as I do about it, and associate it in a friendly way with some of their happiest moments. I feel ashamed when I notice it hanging in a poulterer's shop, and vexed, a little, to see it stuffed in a glass case. In neither circumstances is it the real bird ; it is itself only in its true setting.

It should attract your eye by some slight movement when you are shut off from ordinary things by mist between you and the valley, and are making your way amongst snow-covered boulders ; studying that movement, you should be aware of the scarlet dash above the bird's inquisitive eye, and then pick out its trim white form, so wonderfully blended with those wild surroundings. The ptarmigan is a bold bird, and goes off with no panic. He may deliver a rattling croak or two, then he spreads his wings and sweeps, a white gliding curve against the grey mist, round the shoulder, probably to take up a new stance whence to observe you.

You may see red deer on the Ben ; some say wild goats too, but it has never been my luck to do so.

A story current amongst mountaineers tells how one of them, a devotee of solitude, seeing a couple of figures on a mile-distant skyline, growled to his companion, " There soon won't be room to move on these bally hills." Even if you share his predeliction, you should go up Ben Lomond when Glasgow has a day's holiday in fine weather. You will very likely find the experience quite a social event, for the path may well be—relatively speaking—thronged, and if, on the whole and generally, you like your fellow-creatures, you will enjoy the camaraderie of the occasion, also, by removing or concealing your lunch-litter you may set an example that some will follow. Amongst your fellow-pilgrims you may meet a surprising variety. I hobnobbed one perfect day with a stranger who, as he sat beside on a hot rock and ate his lunch, spoke more about Glasgow's restaurants and their comparative merits, than of the many-coloured glory of the scene outspread for our contemplation. More inspiring was a blind hiker whose friends find him no handicap when tramping, camping and even climbing.

On the last night of April, too, the Ben is often livelier than anyone would expect, for quite a number of enthusiasts mount the path during the hours of darkness—twilight rather if the sky is clear—for the sake of seeing the sunrise. They take their chance, and if their luck is in, their reward is such that ten times the nocturnal discomfort would have been a small price to pay.

Though Ben Lomond is so popular a hill, and though also it has no thousand foot precipice, several accidents have proved that reasonable care should be taken by anybody who leaves the track.

Years ago a missing tourist was long sought all over the mountain, and no clue to his fate found till his body was discovered amongst the rocks in the wooded cleft made by the stream that cuts the western face. It was surmised that he had been short-cutting in a hurry.

More recently an expert climber, taking a photograph from a point on the summit crags, missed his footing and fell to his death. In his memory a cairn with an inscription was erected by his fellow-ramblers well down on the eastern face.

A mountain with no possible dangers is no mountain at all, and of course under certain weather conditions Ben Lomond can be formidable and best left to the experts. There is a sort of comfort for some of us in the fact that an Everest climber was once defeated by Ben Lomond, having tackled it without the equipment appropriate to its ice-capped majesty.

In case any reader is interested, let me mention that the double journey between pier and cairn has been done in one hour fifty-three minutes. This is not fast going, athletically speaking, and for all I know the time has been well beaten. Two hours up and one down is quite good ; but the scenery offers more than ample pretexts for " breathers " which may well stretch this time a hundred per cent.

CHAPTER SIX

ABOVE GLEN FRUIN

THE walk through Glen Fruin, whichever way you take it, is a beautiful one at most seasons, and in its vicinity are others worth tackling when you are in the vein to spend rather more energy than is demanded by the walk straight through.

Make Faslane Bay your starting point. It is strangely transformed since first I knew it. Having tramped from Arrochar, I sat down by the shore, took off my boots and socks and waded in the warm, clear shallows five minutes for the good of my feet. You may not find now a spot for such refreshment just there, but you may discover the lane that runs up the hill, under the railway bridge, and joins the top of the Glen Fruin road near the farm of Strone.

Having reached Strone, pleasant alternatives confront you. The first is to turn due north and follow up the Auchingaich Burn right to its source, cross the watershed at about 1,200 feet, and accept the guidance of another burn which by and bye unites with the Luss Water to bring you down to Loch Lomondside. This is a tougher walk than its length might suggest, and if you do it first, as I did, on a misty day, you may well wonder when you are going to come on any human habitation or definite sign of man's existence. I know that the distances are no less, and the area no more tame in appearance, when the sun shines, but my day was specially lowering, and though I was sure that ultimately I should strike a path developing into a road,

I seemed to walk on and on through the damp cloud as if the map showed what did not in fact exist.

On a brighter day the distant views cheer you on, and you get a wonderful prospect of Loch Lomond and the hills on the farther side.

The second route to which I beg your earnest attention is one I prefer. What I used to do was to set off again up that Auchingaich Burn, but leave it about two miles up and clamber up the steep grass slopes on the right, to find myself in due course on the top of Ben Chaorach (2,338 feet).

From that eminence you see the all-round panorama which makes this walk so superb ; there shine Loch Lomond, Loch Long, the Gareloch and Loch Goil, with a gloriously shaped and coloured tumble of hills amongst them and beyond them in every direction.

Having cooled off and gazed all around, turn south and head for Ben Tharsuinn (2,145 feet). You lose a few hundred feet between the two, but almost all the rest of this walk is downhill, if you disregard the dip between Tharsuinn and the next, slightly higher, crest.

Thinking of the occasions on which I have climbed this Ben Tharsuinn, I remember best a very hot day when I sat to have my lunch there. The sky as well as the out-spread country, with its land and waters, seemed all mine ; I might almost have been adrift in the still, warm air. The detail which remains most distinct in my retrospect is the periodical tap of the wing of a swift on the short dry turf, as the birds dived and zoomed around me, now on my level, now designing marvellous flight-patterns high overhead. Over Balcnock (2,092 ft.) and on to Craperoch, now gently descending, you carry on, accompanied by the same

wide and varied and—you swear—inimitable pageant
of hill and loch and sky, and at last, regretfully even
if you are weary, drop down over Shantron Muir through
the fringe of trees to the Loch Lomond road somewhere
about the point where the road from Helensburgh joins
it.

The rest is anti-climax, whether you avail yourself
of transport or heroically walk on to Alexandria or
Balloch. The redeeming feature of that road, in the
evening of a holiday, is the cavalcade of returning
hikers and cyclists which it stages ; every age and type
is represented, and if your day doesn't make you feel
fraternal to them one and all, you haven't made the
best of it.

The stretch of Loch Lomond road above Luss is
the more interesting to anyone with an eye for the
human contribution to natural beauty. Cynics say
that that contribution is too small to be counted against
human deductions from it—yet when you are coming
down that road at dusk, and see along the shore the
glowing dots which are hiker's tea-fires, and the flame-
tinted smoke drifting into the air amongst the trees,
and against the smooth, dim silver of the loch, surely
you must admit that while they make their tea, these
hardy fellow-creatures are also helping to make a picture
without which your memories of out-door days would
be the poorer.

CHAPTER SEVEN

BETWEEN GLEN DOCHART AND GLEN LOCHAY

SEVERAL high tops here naturally attract the attention of anybody who feels it almost a duty to reach the highest elevations which offer themselves. The four most eminent are Sgiath Chuil (3050 ft.), Meall a' Churain (3,007 ft.), Beinn Chealhaich (3,074 ft.), and Meall Glas (3,139 ft.), the two last being hardly worth regarding as separate tops. All hills are good, but my memory of that group, visited only once, is dulled by the sort of day which luck bestowed upon me.

One of my objects in going there was to enjoy the view of Ben More and its neighbours, which, obviously, could be magnificent. That view was denied me, not by any dramatic interference by snow, rain, or mist, but simply by a sultry, unstirring haze—and that was in May which can so sparkle. The atmosphere was so clogged—that is the word for it—that Ben More was almost invisible across the width of Glen Dochart ; and incidentally so heavy and relaxing that it made me feel lethargic as one feels but seldom a few hundred feet above the valley.

A different kind of day would have given me a totally different impression of this area, and it would be a pity if I discouraged anybody from going to form his own opinion.

To reach to the desired slopes, I crossed the Dochart by a bridge above Glendochart House. Beyond that the burn marked on the map as Allt Riobain comes down from the high beloch on each side of which stand the four tops mentioned above. How you tackle them is a matter for taste, influenced perhaps by the direction of the wind. I took them anti-clockwise, and then thought an interesting way back to Crianlarich would be a bee-line right down to the railway-bridge there. I'm glad I chose that route, for it showed me a stretch of country probably thoroughly characteristic of wide, little-visited areas of the Highlands. I remember, amongst other details, certain flowers that were plentiful up there that July—the butterwort for one, and for another the thrift or sea-pink, that loves also the seashore rocks, and that is familar to everybody who has studied the twelve-sided or "wooden" three-penny bit.

I suppose the mood of the day and the brooding haziness of the atmosphere did a good deal to lend that rough piece of country the air of loneliness and desolation which impressed me. On a clear day it would have seemed very different ; well-known shapes of hills all round would have prevented my feeling as though I must be miles and miles away from anywhere. As it was, I trudged up and down peaty braes, crossed wandering little burns, skirted marshy dips and passed innumerable pools—too diminutive even to call lochans —shut off from the neighbouring heights by the thick, oppressive, enervating mistiness. I might have been on an island, with the sea below instead of Glen Dochart, and no Ben More a few miles away.

That should well be an excellent tramp on a clear day ; on a really bad one, with wind and rain or snow, it seemed to me then that the ground might be impassible.

Ben Chaluim (3,354 ft.) is actually west of the

D

upper part of Glen Lochay, but, being due north of Crianlarich, seems appropriately mentioned here.

The simplest way to approach this hill is to go along the Tyndrum road for about a mile, then cross the river Fillan by the Bridge at Inverhaggernie. Chaluim has no special interest, but is another of those mountains on which height seems easily gained despite the roughish and rather soft going of the lower slopes. It is also a hill which cheats you with false crests, though the real summit is definite enough.

Each of my ascents happens to have been on a hot and brilliant day. On one of those occasions my friend and I postponed our smoke till the top was gained, and there discovered that neither of us had a match; the box we found by the cairn contained not one : our efforts to light a cigarette by the sun's rays through a lens were quite futile.

From the right point, and under the right conditions, Chaluim can wear a sublime beauty which does not depend on its shape. That point is anywhere about Crianlarich village ; the right conditions include a thick covering of snow over the whole landscape, and a brilliant winter dawn. One bitterly cold January morning some of us stood in the snow of the village street hypnotised, almost, by the beauty of the spectacle presented when the top of Chaluim turned rose pink and glowed, above the pallor of the deeply-drifted slopes and ridges leading up to it and still in the shadow of the distant heights over which the unclouded sun was rising. " This beats Switzerland ! " said one of the group, and though he had never been there nobody challenged. At the moment we felt that it could not be beaten, even equalled, anywhere.

CHAPTER EIGHT

THE COBBLER

ONE evening I shared a compartment in the train coming down the side of Loch Long with a stranger, a Scot. The course of the conversation turned to mountaineering, and I was staggered and grieved to hear him say, " Of course there's no rock-climbing in Scotland, is there ? " Even as he made that shocking remark, his head was interrupting my view of the Cobbler with its startling summit.

The Cobbler, like the rest of the " Arrochar Highlands," provides entertainment for every class of " ascender." The person who likes reaching the top of a hill without using his hands finds there a beautiful group of heights to indulge him, and the cragsman is challenged by a great variety of real climbs, some difficult enough for anybody.

Any number of holiday-makers visit Arrochar, and are content to look up at the Cobbler's fantastic summit from the lochside, though it is hard to understand how they resist attempting a nearer view ; still, it is probably as popular a hill as there is in Britain, as far as the more enterprising are concerned. On certain days when Glasgow is on holiday it might be described as frequented, and it has often occurred to me that such a city is astoundingly lucky to have within a few hours' journey a mountain which is in some ways unique.

Why is Ben Arthur called The Cobbler ? Because, you will generally be told, that knob which is the actual summit looks like a man stooping over a last.   Perhaps it does, but the word is more likely to be a corruption of Bein Goblach—"the forked peak," or the peak of the forked Loch, Loch Long's name having been originally Loch Goblach.

No path guides you to the summit, but various routes are obvious.

If you want the shortest and most direct, you can take a car—or 'bus—up Glen Croe, and about three miles up get out and clamber straight up and tackle the steep slope which mounts direct to the " back " of the summit, sparing yourself nearly 400 feet of foot-work.

My favourite route is, I think, the more interesting. I like to leave the highroad just after it rounds the head of the loch, and, skirting the braes, making height all the time, cross the " Buttermilk Burn "—on the map Allt a' Bhalachain—and get on to the rounded ridge which thrusts itself up towards the South Peak. Then —rock-climbing not being on the programme—I skirt that rocky tower, and there I am amongst the crags of the top.

To attain the real tip a little handling of rock is unavoidable, and the last few feet scare some of the less enterprising from ever really conquering the Cobbler at all.   Approaching the " knob " on its eastern side, you see a window or door in the rock ; signs of wear all around indicate that it is open for your passage. Getting through, in a partially folded attitude, you discover yourself on a narrow ledge ; along this you move for a yard or two, hump yourself up a few feet of rock, and there you are on the top slab, which has a slightly sloping surface not much bigger than a big dinner-table. On that you should stand up, and doing so you will feel yourself on a pedestal, and deservedly so.

If you have a " bad head " you may flinch, but, studying the details carefully, you will realise one or two comforting points, the chief of which is that thanks to the drop below it—a drop not far, after all— that ledge gave you a first impression of being far narrower than it is. Actually one man can pass another on it. If the whole performance were to be done without the perspective of the descending slopes all round, you wouldn't think twice about it.

Once upon a time I undertook to escort a party of Boy Scouts up the Cobbler, and took with me a climbing-rope. I knew they would like to be seen in the company of that item of serious equipment, and I meant to use it as a precaution for the last scramble. Our lively party stopped just beside the knob, and I proceeded to knot the rope around the urchin who was to be the pioneer ; by the time the knot was made all his comrades had swarmed through the hole in the rock and were frisking on the summit boulder, one of them yelling to a party of roped climbers on the South Peak, " I hope you'll fall ! "

However, we are not all Boy Scouts. A sturdy youth, resting on the turf below the knob, told me he was content to give the last boulder a miss. His nerve had been shaken by an experience at some similar place where, thrusting through a narrow aperture with a drop behind him, he had forgotten the width of his rucksack, and had been pulled over backwards by it.

I do not recommend a really gusty day for that final tip, nor a day when the whole thing is sheeted in ice or snow ; but others, I know, accept those conditions as introducing a more sporting atmosphere into the climb. It is a matter of taste and capacity and confidence—and equipment. The difference, incidentally, that wet makes to the mica schist rock of which the Cobbler top consists, is well worth taking into account. That beautiful silvery rock can be as slippery as wet ice.

(For anybody who wants to experiment in this matter a big rock called " The Narnain Boulder " may be recommended. It lies beside the Buttermilk Burn, well up, between The Cobbler and Narnain. When it is dry, you can clamber up its side without difficulty, particularly in rubber soles ; when wet, it is a test. The group of boulders in which it is included is well-known amongst the hardier type of hiker and climber, for one of them, happening to be tilted so as to leave a cavity beneath, is popular as a shelter for the night. A rough " dry stone " dyke has been built to afford additional protection, and many a lad whose nights are usually spent under a Glasgow roof can look back on occasionally sleeping there, wakening with the jagged mass of the dawn-crowned Cobbler to greet him ; or, as too often happens, a grey curtain of drenching cloud.)

When the snow is in good condition, several gullies on the east side of the mountain, enclosed in the curve of its crag-battlements, make interesting routes to the top.

Inevitably, considering The Cobbler's situation, the views it commands all round are superb—particularly, perhaps, in winter. One of the most wonderful mountain-spectacles I have ever seen was from its slopes one morning, when snow lay deep and hard on the high ground everywhere. The white peak of Ben

Lomond—from that point of view a shapely cone—
seemed to be hanging high in the sunshine, unsupported,
for a luminous pale haze concealed the lower slopes ;
it was like a mountain in a Chinese painting, unreal, a
mountain and yet more than a mountain, more significant beyond anything material.

The man who was with me was new to the Cobbler,
and as soon as we had kicked our way up the steep
drift round the base of the South Peak, he scrambled
hurriedly to the edge of the beautiful glittering bank
that ran up to the brink of the corrie, and peered over.
He is definitely not one of those blessed with " a head
for heights," and the startled expression of his face,
as he as hastily withdrew, has been a joke between us
ever since ; he had found himself on the lip of a cornice,
gazing down into a white gulf that gave the momentary
impression of being an almost infinite abyss. I have
thought that some of the old-fashioned descriptive
writers provided posterity with such first impressions,
not with more leisurely realizations of the facts.

The Cobbler is an inexhaustible hill for all sorts of
people, the botanist amongst them. Its lower slopes
are always wet, even in drought, and botanists know
what that means for them. The Rose-root, to which I
refer in connection with Ben Lui, loves the damp rocks
around the corrie, and the Purple Orchis is another
flower, which, in its season, flourishes with lavish abun-
dance lower down.

If you are filled with a sense of achievement
when you stand erect on the Cobbler's unusual
summit, feeling yourself deserving of your pedestal,
you may also, by the time you have nearly
reached the road on your return, experience the appro-

priate sense of satisfaction, for it can seem a long way down. It is pleasant then to see, cast by the evening light on the white, green, or tawny slopes on the far side of the loch, the shadow-silhouette of the craggy summit you are leaving to the night.

It seems a pity, perhaps, that The Cobbler falls short of the rank of a " Munro," as it does by just over a hundred feet ; yet if you are fanciful you may think of it like some of those great commoners who seem all the greater because they scorned a title.

THE SUMMIT OF THE COBBLER

W.K.H

CHAPTER NINE

MORE HILLS AROUND ARROCHAR

THE Cobbler is not the only worthy hill associated with Arrochar, not by any means, even if that remarkable mountain has here received a chapter to itself. Within the " lozenge " formed by Glen Loin, Glen Sloy, the Kinglas Water, and Glen Croe is contained as interesting a cluster of fascinating heights of which I am one of many who never tire. And that lozenge is surrounded by others of almost equal quality.

Ben Ime (3,318 feet) is the highest, as well as the centre of the group, and if only for the sake of the view from the top should be climbed one of the first. From that point of vantage the prospector can get a clear idea of the lay-out of the whole of the " Arrochar Highlands." One way of climbing Ben Ime is from about the Butter Bridge—I understand that Ben Ime means the Butter Mountain, though why, nobody seems to know—just where the Kinglas Water turns west to run towards Loch Fyne. The aspect of Ben Ime from here is quite imposing, and the ascent steep. My usual route is from the other side. I start as if for the Cobbler, but instead of crossing the Allt a' Bhalachain, or Buttermilk Burn, follow it right up under the steep south front of Narnain, passing the Narnain Boulder, night-shelter for the hardy, and across the marshy watershed whence that dashing torrent leaves its cradle amongst mosses that are always beautiful. Turning there to the right, you see before you the long easy slope to the top of Ben Ime. Crags fringe the eastern

47

side, but your path is mostly grass till close to the summit. Ime has a sort of double top ; the cairn is on the one further north.

It is one the biggest and most solidly-built cairns I know, with a flat top on which—in the right weather— it is pleasant to sprawl and bask, revolving now and then to absorb something, at least, of the largesse of mountain scenery outspread at all points of the compass. Such views can be almost hypnotic. I remember one afternoon in early spring sitting up there watching the sunset and the effects of the after-glow, forgetful of the time. The upper slopes of all the hills were white ; the surface of the lochs, shadowed from the western radiance by their enclosing heights, a mysterious dark green ; their distance below me was exaggerated by the sombre colour and vague shapes of the lower slopes. I seemed, up there, to be above the reach of darkness. Remembering at length that I was a good long way from anywhere and had better move, I started downhill, and soon left the light of the after-glow behind me.

The last stage of the descent—cutting across the lower slopes of Narnain en route for Succoth at the head of Loch Long—demanded a certain amount of care. The moon was up, and as she brightened, more potent became her cold and lovely witchcraft, transforming familiar things, casting deceptive shadows, glittering from every little pool. That hillside is broken with very characteristic miniature precipices ; with the moon in my eyes I found it difficult to spot these, for they were indistinguishable from their surroundings, and I had to move slowly lest I should step over one of them and get at least a nasty jar.

Narnain (3,036 ft.) is a hill craggy enough to please

anybody, which may be said also of A Chrois (2,765 ft.).
For a good rough walk amongst wild and rocky surroundings, with unlimited practice in scrambling
amongst assorted boulders, I suggest the ascent of
Narnain straight up the long shoulder from Succoth,
keeping to the left as you approach the top. Of course
there are rock climbs up there ; perhaps the best known,
a short one, excellent for beginners, is the Spearhead
Arrete. Then there is the Jammed Block Chimney,
more complicated, and though I do not mean to intrude
upon the cragsman's sphere, I must record a memory
of one winter afternoon when a party of us scrambled
up through mist and over snow-muffled rocks, with a
rope, thinking we might do that little climb. To start
it you enter the bottom of a great sheer-sided split in
the rocks, then clamber on to the uppermost of several
great boulders. From that point there are two ways
to emerge ; one is above you through an opening suited
only for the slim ; the other, less constricting but
airier, is out through the split on to the crag face, then,
turning round, with what seems to the novice a long
drop at your back, over the edge not far above. It
sounds, looks, and for the expert really is, quite easy,
but the last bit of the scramble offers a trap in the form
of a notch in the cliff-edge. It is such a notch as tempts
the inexpert, who feels that he would be safer with his
body in it than worming over the uncompromising
straight rim of the rock hard by. It is a trap, however,
because once it gets you into it, it does its best to hold
you wedged.

That day was voted by the majority of the party
quite unsuitable for exploits. The wind was howling
and icy, the mist thick, and everything disguised and

treacherous with ice and snow. (Your real rock-climber will laugh—such conditions are his delight, but we were inspired by the better part of valour.) Refusing to encourage even one of our accompanying experts to lead, we decided on a compromise. One took the rope, descended from the boulder-top, and made his way to the summit of the crag by the ordinary scrambler's route. Then, with an absolutely secure stance for himself and unlimited choice of belays for the rope, he flung its end down to us, and one by one we completed the brief gymnastic effort and joined him. When my turn came, though I thought I was avoiding the lure of the above-mentioned notch, it got me. I was thickly clad, and there I stuck. The man with the rope, well back from the cliff's edge, had me safe, duly taking in every inch of slack that developed as I struggled to extricate myself, and thoroughly enjoying the look on my face as I wriggled and hauled and heaved and grew redder and redder until at length I escaped and squirmed out on to the level at the top.

I mention this incident partly to indicate what the rope can mean, and what it is for. It means moral support ; I was perfectly happy, despite the long drop at my back, and could use my muscles with an easy mind. My friend holding it didn't haul me—he was enjoying the fun, and also knew that I wanted to extricate myself under my own power ; but he made the rope serve as a safeguard.

Perhaps I never spent a merrier afternoon than that. As we sat waiting for the end of the rope to appear, a little group huddled on the top of a big boulder in a rock cleft through which the wind was keening, with a view of nothing but ice and black rock and snow seen through wan mist, I suppose if "televised" for the benefit of friends sitting at home at ease we should have made a picture of wretchedness, but I know that we were in hilarious spirits. That seemed just the right place for us.

Returning towards Arrochar, trying glissades where the slope and the snow encouraged them, we were startled to see the leading man turn a beautiful Catherine Wheel—he claimed a double one—as a consequence of getting his legs entangled with his ice-axe. Anybody less tough would have broken his neck, but he rose from the snow, shook himself, and discovered that he was none the worse. (Once, by a less spectacular glissading spill, I set off a box of matches in a pocket, and later discovered that the lining was burned out, and then understood the nature of the most peculiar odour I had wondered about just after my somersault.)

A Chrois is to me a mysterious mountain on account of the remarkable fissures across its easterly slopes, fissures like crevasses. Some of them are said to be sixty feet deep. A story is told of a sheep-dog which fell or found its way into one and which was eventually spared death from starvation by a piece of poisoned meat dropped down to it by its owner who had tried in vain to rescue it. Some of these clefts can be entered from below and studied. Some narrow quite gradually at one end, so that you could step across them, and I suggest that anybody moving about that face of A Chrois in the dusk, or when the hill is snow-covered, would be wise to use caution.

Many boulders there seem to cover other fissures of considerable depth ; a stone, pushed into some small crevice at the side, may be heard " stotting " down in the most suggestive fashion.

A Chrois is not the only mountain near Arrochar which has queer fissures ; Ben an Lochain, above Loch Restil, has some, and some startling crags too ; the crags about the top of Ben Donich, west of Glen Croe, look as if they had all received a great sideways heave at some time, and the Brack also has detail worth investigation.

Both those—Donich and the Brack—well repay a visit. The former is for me associated with a disappointment I cannot forget.

It happened on a sultry afternoon when I had first climbed Ben an Lochain, then dropped down to Glen More, crossed the road and toiled up Donich. I was desperately hot, and going downhill, fast, was more heating than going up. The sun had no mercy, and there was no hint of breeze to fan my broiling skin. Looking down through the glowing air, I observed a spectacle that filled me with hope ; was not that a picnic party strewn by the road-side in Glen Croe ? Could I not see the light frocks of girls—white, red ? Well, if I made my descent so that I had to pass them on the road, was there not a chance that a cup of tea would be offered to the poor chap, obviously being roasted alive, who should plod past the spot where a kettle was boiling and kind hearts beating ?

My picnic party underwent a dreary transformation as I made downhill towards it ; the sympathetic girls in gay-hued frocks changed into nothing less prosaic and unresponsive than painted tar-barrels, dumped by a road-making gang !

So all that I had to swallow in Glen Croe was cold

water—a very little was best, for my temperature must have turned it to steam instantaneously—and my disappointment. Luck, however, relented, and I was presently offered, and accepted, a lift into Arrochar.

I am not amongst the pedestrians who have a standing quarrel with the man in the car, partly because I am sometimes that man myself, while he may be a hiker at heart, or even a mountaineer. I have been offered lifts when they were most welcome, and begged them when they have got me out of a time-jam. I have also declined them, and enjoyed the bewilderment of the well-intentioned driver. It is pleasant to be able to recall the fact that I was once lifted by the police in one of their radio cars. That was one terrific evening on the Fenwick Moor road. A sudden blizzard had come on, and a long line of Glasgow-bound buses including mine was held up by a huge tractor which had skidded and lay immovable across the road. It was cold in the 'bus, with no definite news of rescue in any form, and I decided to start walking. To have got anywhere worth while would have taken a mighty long time, for I found the conditions really savage, with drifts piling along the road and the snow flying horizontally before a furious wind. Ploughing through the deepening drifts and staggering to the buffets of the shrieking gusts, I had not made much headway when a vehicle loomed through the flurry and a voice said, " You'd better get in." I heartily agreed, and was transported to the city's fringe and the car-lines, safe in the hands of the police. A cynic might say that it was obviously less trouble for them to bring me back alive than to have to search for my frozen corpse, amongst the drifts : those drifts, whipped and scored and sculptured by the gale, made in the morrow's sunshine a spectacle that enterprising lovers of unusual sights thought well worth a journey to see.

Also I have been in cars over-crowded with hikers collected as they trudged hopefully in the direction of far-distant homes, and the physical discomfort has had its compensations in the sense of camaraderie and the interest of others' experiences.

At the same time, let me confess, I have known that attitude of pitying superiority towards the people cooped up in travelling boxes when I was moving in the open air and the rain, warm by internal combustion while they were huddled in a fug. Is it not a little pathetic to see, as one may on a wet day in Glen Croe, cars halted in the downpour at the roadside, full of people waiting till the Primus boils their kettle, or drinking their tea from a vacuum flask, and imagining that they were having an afternoon in the country— amongst the mountains—when you are on your pedestrian way to, or from, some cloud-hidden hill-top ? " Just motorists" we are apt to think, even as at other times, looking down on pigmy figures pottering about trimmed areas approaching the first slopes, we have been known to comment to one another, " Mere golfers." We must not cultivate this attitude of superiority. It is generally quite temporary, and induced by the conditions of the moment. Next day we may ourselves be car-borne or concentrating on a putt. I mention it simply as an indication of one of the curious effects of hard exercise at altitudes above that of one's habitat.

Amongst the easier hills around Arrochar is Ben Reoch (2,168 ft.), which commands what I have heard

eulogised as the finest view of any height in the neighbourhood. Access may be obtained from anywhere
along the Tarbet-Arrochar road, of which the hill rises
due south. Its top is broken and interesting, and on
its northern face are some odd caves and crevices,
tempting to explore. I was amused once to find my
intrusion resented by, of all monsters, a tomtit, which
hung about uttering protests and, presumably, menaces,
while I investigated the beauties of rock and fern and
moss in that cleft, with its wide roof of slanting rock.

For a change, anybody staying at Arrochar should
make his way to Ardlui, and walk up Glen Falloch to
Crianlarich—or preferably reverse the procedure, not
only because it is easier to walk downhill, but because
the opening vista down Loch Lomond is the view to
have ahead. To me there is something particularly
attractive about that whole glen ; the northern end
is given a special character by its groups of pines, and
the plunge of the hillsides down from the east offers
some really fine spectacles.

Not far above the head of Loch Lomond a bridge
crosses the Falloch, almost opposite the long cascade
of the Ben Glas burn, which can be superb in wet weather.
The presence of that convenient bridge may induce you
to cross it and from that direction tackle some of the
big hills of the grand group of which Ben More is the
sovereign. It is a most interesting approach, but one
demanding plenty of patience and a certain reserve of
stamina. My impression is that the climber from Glen
Falloch is confronted with lines of strata running across
his route instead of with it, so that his progress is
perpetually up and down over a succession of ridges.
By the time you have reached the top of Ben Chabhair

E

(3,053 ft.) from this direction, you will think you have
climbed twice that height. Nevertheless, all that high
area is most interesting, with plenty of wild scenery
around, and if you are really ready for some pretty
steep switchbacks you may take your pick of a variety
of descents towards other points of the Glen. Look
at your map and notice the long ridges, rock-fringed
but themselves easy walking, outspread like fingers ;
are not those two from An Caesteal attractive in their
suggestion—the one that runs over the lower crest of
Stob Glas, and the other with its unexpected name of
Twistin Hill ?

That steep face above the bridge at Benglass Farm
is associated for me with a strangely incongruous
figure encountered there, one blazing, baking July
day. Sitting amongst the heather and the ferns, the
bog myrtle and the mosses and the shattered
rocks, was an individual in a black suit and a bowler
hat, who looked as if he must have been transported
straight from a Glasgow smoke-room.

His presence was explained by the vasculum he
carried ; he was one of a botanizing party, sensible
enough to sit down to rest and cool while the others
toiled ahead. A specialist in mosses, he had assuredly
attained a happy hunting-ground. As to his attire,
I suppose that was explained either by lack of experience
of climbing in August or by that devotion to the bowler
hat which amounts to a principle—or did till a few
years ago—amongst some of the older generation of
Glasgow men. To me a bowler hat on a mountain is
tantamount to sacrilege. However, we had a pleasant
chat in that lovely spot, and then I in my shirt and
shorts bade a comradely farewell to him in his sombre

felt dome and office suit. We were both happy, so what else mattered ?

Another admirable Arrochar walk is that right round Ben Vorlich down to the bottom of Glen Falloch. it is a long twelve miles or more, and parts of it pretty rough. You start by a path up Glen Loin, then follow up the Inveruglas Water, pass Loch Sloy in its narrow gully—notice the steep slopes either side, and mark them down for a vigorous day—and then, after passing Loch Sloy Farm, practise a little route-finding over the water-shed till you reach the start of the burn named Srath Dubh-uisge ; the fact is the slopes hem you in so that you are hardly likely to wander.

How this area has been transformed since it was decided that the waters of Loch Sloy must be made to work! Glen Loin can be so beautiful that to regard it only as the route for somewhere else would be a pitiful mistake. Its lower portion is a narrow level little valley between steep mountainsides, and in the right kind of weather has an atmosphere of verdant serenity extremely pleasant and encouraging to an idling mood. The purple crags look challenging and stern ; here in spring, while snow still clings above, are warm sunshine, birdsong, and hosts of primroses. Another most rewarding walk in this inexhaustible neighbourhood is through Glen Douglas to Loch Lomond. The road can be cycled, but is not too " good " for the pedes-trian's pleasure. I passed that way early one marvellous summer morning, and thought some enchantment had been worked, for Ben Lomond and all the eastern shore had vanished—before me was nothing but the glitter of smooth water. All else was lost in golden heat haze.

Arrochar is a good centre for what I call exploring in miniature, the pastime of a lazy day, or the resource of the lover of wild beauty debarred by any reason from seeking it far afield and at the expense of ample energy. Even if you are a peak-bagger and a rock-gymnast, try the experiment of devoting a few hours to the investigation in detail of any one of the burns that tumble from the heights. Take it slowly, for they come down slopes that have a good steep angle. Pick the Sugach burn, which comes so triumphantly down past Succoth Farm. (The similarity of those names has always worried me ; which came first ? Which is a corruption of the other ?) That burn has beauty every yard of its way ; in the course of time it has made its own scenery—its cliffs, linns, water-slides ; and flowers, mosses, growing things in fascin-ating variety, find a congenial habitat in its moist neighbourhood. Heather and bluebells, primroses, dog violets, bog myrtle, bog asphodel, butterwort, orchids—I am no botanist, and these are only a few of the decorations that fringe the little gorges, with here and there a rowan for dignity. In spate the Sugach is no miniature torrent at all, but a furious rush with an impetuous roar of its own ; for your first exploration choose a day when it is small, not so hurried, and singing its fine-weather music.

If you are energetic and follow it right up to its springs, you will be rewarded, for you will find yourself in the Sugach Corrie, a surprising marshy amphitheatre ringed by impressive rock-battlements.

Any of the burns around will reward intensive study, whatever your particular nature-interest may be. One might, I fancy, develop for their exploration an

enthusiasm almost as possessive as that for the hills
themselves. What overwhelming grandeurs, I have
sometimes thought as I studied some three-foot precipice with its dark tiny linn below, for a Lilliputian
wanderer !

CHAPTER TEN

AN AFTERNOON ON CRUACH TARBET

THIS, which is amongst the hills around the head of Loch Long but not of the distinguished, is no hill for the ambitious. It stands just at the back of Arrochar, the houses of which are indeed upon its slopes, with gardens that in hard winters suffer the depredations of the deer. Arrochar for most of us means the Cobbler and the rest of that irresistible group, but it is worth while devoting an hour or two to this modest hill, only some 1,400 feet high, if only because it holds you aloft to look at its nobler neighbours.

One of my visits was on a March afternoon, and the time was not wasted. The hill is distinguished from below by a sort of false crest topped by a rock with an overhang presenting a rather imposing silhouette just as though it were a quite important summit. The view, even from there, justifies this pose, though from the true top, some distance back, it is far finer. From it you obtain a magnificent picture of Ben Vorlich and Ben Vane, with a glimpse of Loch Sloy in the narrow glen between them. The explorer is, however, likely to be most impressed by the view of the crest of Ben Lomond, whose serrated summit ridge looks from here like a pyramidal peak, and is really impressive when graced by snow cornices ; and the unexpected vista both up and down Loch Lomond with its strewn green islands is another of the entertainments offered by this little hill.

Cruach Tarbet is richly decorated by groups of

great shattered rocks, of the typically schistose type, which gleams a beautiful silver-grey when wet. At that time of year the greater area of the hill wore the colour of brown velvet ; and when there trotted across my front eight big stags the resemblance of their hue to that of their background was remarkable ; in their coats seemed blent the hues of marsh-grass, withered bracken, and mosses. The hill that day was populous with deer and mountain hares, the latter in all stages between their summer and their winter colouring. The hares seemed very tame ; one allowed me to approach near enough to see that it was in extremely poor condition before loping off with that marvellous gait known to no other creature.

(On Carn Mhor Dearg I once patted a hare ; the poor beast was little but skin and bone, though the month was August, and I suppose it was too ill to be afraid even of man.)

Of course there were grouse also, and against the blur of a raincloud advancing from the veiled head of Narnain came soaring a big bird that ought to have been a Golden Eagle, but which I cannot in honesty claim. (Why are we all so suspicious of other men's eagles ? They cannot all be buzzards. My own scepticism may have been founded by a report, published years ago, of an attack by an eagle on a child in a perambulator not far from Menstrie, and its sequel. The young woman in charge said it was a golden eagle, and that it would not be lured away from the pram even by the offer of a sweet biscuit. The bird was later claimed by its late owner as a strayed tame jackdaw).

When the rain-squall arrived, I moved round to the lee of the hill and realised once more how pleasant is relative calm after the bullying and hullabaloo of such stormy demonstrations. Even on that unpleasant afternoon—so it was, really, from any standpoint but that of those who don't like out-of-door conditions ever called unpleasant with no qualification—even then there was a store of beauty, near and far, to entertain me. The landscape was rich in strong hues—reds and purples and vivid greys, and now and then the untidy clouds were torn apart to allow the sun to glorify for a few minutes some distant brae or group of leafless trees, or that imposing tip of Ben Lomond, assuming the dignity of remoteness as wisps of cloud blurred it intermittently. No wonder, perhaps, that there are people who claim that Ben Lomond is Scotland's highest mountain. He has an air of his own, and no rivals close enough for comparison. Also, those who never climbed any other hill, and have no intention of ever doing so, have been led by their own physical sensations, the day after the adventure, to believe that no other hill could possibly have such an interminable altitude !

As I descended in the teeth of the wet bluster, I saw a movement on the brae below. Thirty or forty deer were gathered there ; every head was turned my way, every animal in an attitude of intense vigilance. Such concentration of interest is almost embarrassing to the solitary intruder, and deer are not the only animals which will bring to bear upon a human suspect. I have been stared at by sheep, several score of them drawn up in line as I walked along a brae, in a way that suggested their intention of comparing notes in no very complimentary strain, as soon as this biped was off their pasture.

For a moment the deer watched, motionless, then on a common impulse walked off to disappear round a shoulder. Changing direction and getting my camera ready, I tried to outflank them, but their sentinel saw me and again they were off. Time after time this happened, and I had to let them win, my final reflection about that makeshift afternoon being that if anyone wants fresh air and exercise, and would also play a part typifying man's pursuit of the ideal, he should go stalking deer with a camera, on a wind-swept, rain-soaked little hill like Cruach Tarbet.

CHAPTER ELEVEN

TULLICH HILL, AND SNOW

TULLICH HILL is by no means amongst the famous. It is only 2,075 feet in height, with nothing to attract the climber except that it is a hill, and has one of the best obtainable views of the Arrochar Highlands. It stands on the east side of Loch Long, opposite the Brack, and the most simple route by which to get at it is to walk down the line from Arrochar and then go ahead. Naturally, being in that locality, it is a dampish hill, but it has its rocky outbreaks here and there, and is quite worth an afternoon's attention.

I enjoyed Tullich Hill most on a certain day when the conditions were what might, had they not been defied, have been called horrible. Snow covered everything, but a thaw had set in, with clouds on the tops and wet in the wind.

Rather than idle grumbling by the fire, our small party, in clothes fit only for what we had in mind, scrambled and ploughed and slithered our way up in to the damp grey cloud ; saw that there was nothing else to be seen, and then came down again, glissading, either on our feet or the seats of our trousers, or at full length, wherever the slope and the state of the snow encouraged that form of progress. As glissading it was not thrilling, but it was great fun, and our sopping condition made dry clothes and comfort the height of luxury.

That was not snow at its best ; it was indeed what I find that most completely urban-minded people

consider snow in general to be—cold, wet, and associated with chilblains. I feel urged to say a little about
snow as we know it on the hills.

To begin with, then, snow on the hills is something
entirely different from the stuff that has to be carted
off city streets after a fall. That might be called
" dead " snow—a complete contrast to the living,
sparkling substance that makes even the most familiar
hill new and wonderful. As for associating it primarily
with cold—I do not find that natural to my reminiscent
mind. Admittedly I have been chilled to the marrow
amongst it, but that was when it was melting, and on
the other hand I have been as hot while toiling over its
sun-reflecting frozen surface, or labouring through dry,
knee-deep drifts, as on any midsummer day.

What colour is snow ? The probably commonest
answer would be " White "—possibly " Grey." Real
observation of it, seen at its best, discovers that it has
all the colours of the rainbow, jewel-bright. As you
walk across a frozen drift under a clear sky, without any
of the valley's haze to dim the brilliance of the details
around, you see an infinity of sparks dazzling from the
smooth surface, as though you were treading a solid
mass of microscopic diamonds. From the valley the
loose snow on the hilltops may sometimes be seen
blowing like scattered white smoke. That is a pretty
enough spectacle from a distance, but those gale-driven
clouds of snow dust are cruel to face—and will make
you keep your eyes too nearly closed to see anything
beyond your next step. If the snow is very hard, a
strong wind can create a most curious effect by driving
particles in a hurrying haze perhaps no more than a
foot above the frozen surface. I remember watching

a field mouse trying to progress through such a miniature blizzard—no miniature to that tiny scrap of life !— and being from time to time blown right head over heels. What brought the creature out in such weather ?

As for the beauty of the forms which snow assumes under the drive of the wind, no pen could do them justice. In the mass and in detail those forms are equally marvellous—the curve of the great drift, with its surface graven into waves or furrows ; the lovely grace of the long cornice hanging over its own blue shadow, and the feather-fine edge of the snow ripples and breakers. As for that blue of the shadows amongst high snow, I do not know of any name for it. You see glimpses of something like it in some of the pictures by the old Italian masters, but paint could never reproduce that celestial luminosity. No matter how clear the atmosphere, the valleys are always more or less haunted by vapour, as you realise when looking down into them from the heights, and that vapour must, however slightly, dim the radiance of sun-reflecting snow, and dull the colour of the shadows cast upon it. Above the haze, you see it as nowhere else ; the heavenly blue fills every mark made by your boots on the bright surface.

To be high on a snow-covered hill when the sun is setting in a flare of gold and crimson is to enjoy a colour-spectacle startling in its contrasts ; the shadow that brims a deep footmark then reveals its purple-blue all the more strongly for the warm glow of the unbroken surface. Of course, I am told that " retinal fatigue " creates many strange colour-effects ; I am not for the moment interested in the cause.

Perhaps I have never seen that sunset-splendour

better than one evening on White Wisp in the Ochils. The friend who was with me had brought his cairn terrier Bodach with him : the snow proved just a little too soft and deep for Bodach on the slopes, and we took turns in carrying him draped across our shoulders.   A Cairn terrier grows surprisingly heavy after a time, but, worn so, may be recommended for keeping the back of the neck warm and cosy.   Reaching the summit of the hill, which is flattish, we let Bodach experiment under his own power.   The crust was harder up there, and would have borne his weight, but Bodach seemed to think that as a good dog he must follow exactly in our trail ; this meant that half the time he was partially hidden in the big holes left by every step we made, tumbling into those wells of heavenly colour, and emerging to scramble into the next, amidst snow reflecting the awe-inspiring conflagration in the west ; seldom, surely, can a hot little dog's efforts have had a background more superb.

Snow can become a quite absorbing study.   Many a year ago I was a little puzzled to hear an Everest climber say that after due experience the mountaineer could form a fair idea whether or not a snow-bridge would bear his weight, merely by looking at it.

Gradually I have learned to understand what he meant, and to realise that the beginnings of snow-lore may be acquired on quite humble hills, so that after a time you can form a fairly good idea whether you will sink into or walk over, or skid on and go sliding down the drift before your eyes. The texture of the surface varies, and those variations are all significant.   It is amusing, too, to think out what processes a drift in a particular position has passed through since the fall of the snow that made it. How did it fall ? From which direction, and has it been beaten by days of high wind, or half-melted and frozen again ? One side of a gully may have had more sun than the other during the day, so that for some hours the drift that fills it will be softer that side than the other ; but soon after the evening frost sets in it will be very much the harder.

You may have little chance of becoming a real snow-expert, but you can enjoy an industrious apprenticeship without going very far afield, and find that every item of knowledge on the subject—as in the case of botany, geology, and ornithology—gives a new interest to your mountain walks.

Snow is perhaps at its " queerest " under a heavy sky, when there is not sufficient definite light to cast even the ghost of a shadow. It is impossible, under those conditions, to judge the level of the surface immediately in front ; at the next pace you may find yourself stepping a foot down, or that your boot collides with a foot-high rock.

(In that fascinating and awe-inspiring book *War Below Zero*, one of its writers refers to the bewilderment caused to the men on duty in Greenland by shadowless snow ; he says that a man who had stooped to pick up something sometimes fell over backwards, just because there was no way in which his eye could make that instinctive judgment of angles ; the man could not tell when he was perpendicular to the surface).

One other thing I must remark on this subject ; if you are interested in the details of hills, and in particular such details as ancient tracks and the sites of old buildings, you will find snow a helpful collaborator in your researches.   As a deep fall melts, its last remains often make most interesting revelations, lingering longest in sheltered depressions, and calling your attention to details that tell some story of the past— or that at least hint at stories long forgotten.

Probably I have said enough about snow.   I am enthusiastic for its beauty and its wonder, and should like those who misjudge it to enjoy some of the delight of mind and body which, in one way and another, it has afforded me—snow, from the tiny " filigree petal " to the far-flung splendour glorifying a whole mountain range.

CHAPTER TWELVE

AROUND BEN NEVIS

THE greater includes the less, and some who have
reached the top of Scotland's highest mountain
appear to believe that in virtue of that feat all the
country's peaks are part of their conquest. They have
been where nobody, with his feet on the ground, can
look down on them. That is a pleasing fancy which
perhaps encourages not a few as they toil up the
ascending stony zigzags of the path that leads to the
cairn from Achintee Farm—the furthest point to which,
normally, a car can be taken. (I say normally, for on
several occasions, by hook or by crook, cars have got
to the top. So, long ago, has a wheelbarrow, propelled
or dragged by some enthusiast who was no doubt amply
rewarded by being able afterwards to say that he had
done it).

Frankly, it is a weary trudge, but the inexperienced
and the scorners of advice find it worse than they need.
For the sake of your feet, go heavily shod. If your soles
are thin, you may well share the sentiment of a lady
overheard to say to her companion, as with flinching
steps they approached the car awaiting their return to
Achintee, " I never want to see a stone again."

If you start with high heels you are likely to finish
without them. The number of scraps of rubber sole
and detached heels which, in the tourist season, can
be collected on the path, tell their own tale of needless
martyrdom.

What you should wear are soles through which the

R.K.H.

BEN NEVIS, FROM CORPACH

pressure of the individual stone is not perceptible. For the feet the descent is the worse ordeal, because the hot and weary toes are jammed forward at every step.

Let me here remark that women on mountains often seem free from the tyranny of certain natural laws to which men are subject. Regarding footwear they are particularly mysterious. I have seen a lady, dressed and shod as for Princes Street, strolling up that path with not a hair out of place. I believe she was carrying a sunshade, and she reached the top, which is more than can be said for some who start more appropriately equipped.

Perhaps her success, and her coolness, were due to the very fact that she was just strolling, while the failures were scurrying in bursts punctuated by long rests. The first time I escorted my sister up Ben Nevis she thought me a dictatorial handicap, because I kept insisting on a slower pace, and a bully because I discouraged rests, but we got to the top long before parties who had started before us.

My recommendation is for the steady plod, and enjoyment of the scenery while you are on the move.

Obviously this is not advice for anybody who is out to see how fast he can do the mountain. It was no " plodding " which won the Nevis record in 1939, when one Mulholland went up and down in 2 hrs. 3 mins., 43 seconds. That seems to me one of the most astounding of athletic feats. The distance from Fort William Post-office to the summit and back is fourteen miles—reduced a little, to be sure, by the short cuts possible on the descent—and the rise 4,406 feet. Many years ago a feminine postman, or postwoman, did the ascent in two hours, and anybody who equals that may

F

consider himself in good form. As to such speed trials
on hills, some hill-lovers think them almost sacrilegious,
and unworthy of a true mountaineer. I do not see the
force of the argument. Such feats, I acknowledge,
have nothing to do with mountaineering, but belong to
a branch of athletics. Why frown on them any more
than on cross-country running or track-racing ?

An athlete is a fool if he does not know when to
stop and when a feat is beyond him, and I do not see
why the young and fit should not let off steam by now
and then dashing up a mountain, experiencing the
exhilaration of a really all-out effort amidst grand
surroundings.

Well, such dashes are not for everybody. Discussion of them leads to heated argument in many
circles, and can therefore bring out some interesting
points of view.

For the average walker I should say that four hours
up and three down make reasonable timing, but if the
weather is good a summer day is hardly too long—if
you don't mind carrying appropriate supplies. (Attaché
cases and baskets are to be seen on that path. The
awkwardness of these tempts to intermittent picnics
en route, and these in turn induce disinclination to
proceed. There is nothing like the rucksack, of course).

Once upon a time, when the Observatory was still
operating, the summit had its Hotel or refreshment-
room. Nothing of that is left, but the solid walls of
the observatory still stand. A drink of water at the
Hotel cost 6d., but, for those who could find it, there
was a spring just below the top on the western side.

The burden of a vacuum flask of hot tea—or better,
perhaps, soup—will be forgotten if you find the summit

enshrouded in clammy cloud, or with sleet falling, as it sometimes does even in August.

Some hill-ramblers, and I am one of them, get into the habit of going all day, even in hot weather, without drinking at all. Perhaps it is a mistaken habit, and we should be wiser to keep replacing the liquid which exertion uses up. Other veterans are sippers, drinking by the rule of little and often. Dogmatism is not called for—though " Often and lots " may certainly be deprecated as a guiding principle.

I have climbed with some men who thought it worth while to carry with them a big tin of fruit, apricots or peaches, and such a luxury makes a delightful finish to a sandwich meal, particularly if, on a really hot day, there is to be found in some cranny a lingering drift which can contribute a dash of snow to top each mouthful of fruit.

Every walker must decide for himself between the advantages of going light and eating luxuriously. Emergencies may arise, or he may be attacked by an unusual fit of hunger. That observation brings me back to Ben Nevis.

I had started one day after lunch, planning to push hard and to be back for tea, and so I took not so much as a biscuit. It was a bleak, damp, windy afternoon, and on the summit I suddenly felt furiously hungry. Various odds and ends are apt to litter that plateau during tourist-time ; on that occasion they included two unwrapped sandwiches, reposing as if placed by some very tidy person on a boulder overlooking the cliffs.

Accustomed to a Glasgow quick-lunch rendezvous where a notice used to request customers when making their choice not to handle the sandwiches " more than is necessary," I was not the man to be fussy, and regarding somebody's abandoned surplus as a kind of fairy reward for visiting Nevis on such a day, I grabbed a sandwich and took a brave bite. Fairy gift indeed ! Yes, just such a gift as the Good Folk—the malicious creatures of the "Secret Commonwealth"—would love to play on an intruding mortal. The filling of those sandwiches was fat cold mutton, and exposure to the rain and the wind had robbed meat and bread alike of all flavour, and left only soft and loathsome texture.

One bite sufficed to cure my hunger.

After this digression, back to the ascent. Naturally a settled fine day is best for the first time, and naturally you want a good view from the top. Remember that a warm, still day often means haze. Also that conditions may change drastically between sea-level and an elevation of four thousand feet, so that even at the height of summer there is no predicting what conditions you may encounter as you climb. I have seen the flame of a match lighted on the top stand unwavering " like the candles on a shrine," also the desecration of an umbrella, unshaken beneath a steady windless drizzle, and in the same month have been greeted by sleet-squalls.

Bear all this in mind when deciding what clothes to carry.

It has been stated that in the summer of 1945, for the first time in living memory, snow entirely disappeared from the summit. I daresay I am not the only old frequenter of Nevis who hugs the belief that had he tried he could have found a capful in some crack ; at any rate, in my experience, it has never been anything like snow-free. In June or July you may find solid masses of frozen snow inside the shell of the Observatory, and big drifts sloping down the gullies.

Even if cloud is resting on the summit, you may have glorious views as you ascend, for mountains and lochs are all around. Glimpses of sunlit hills and waters between masses of drifting grey cloud have a brilliance of colouring which makes them seem to belong to a world even more beautiful than the one with which you are familiar.

Dirty weather, even in summer, can of course be definitely uncomfortable at such an elevation, and yet, though conditions are deteriorating as you go up, I advise you to persevere. Why waste the energy already invested in the enterprise ? In any case you will have an experience satisfactory in retrospect, and you may be one of those who discover an eerie beauty in the drift and eddying of cloud-wreaths, and in the march of advancing rain-curtains. And you may be thrilled to listen to the hollow, mysterious voices of the wind, charging the hidden crags below.

And the more uncomfortable you are on your mountains the more blissful the contrast when you return to base and feel entitled to every luxury it can produce. I recall the satisfaction on the face of a pretty girl as she crouched before the fire in a Fort William hotel. She herself had changed and was glowing, and she was drying several £1 notes which had been in her purse in a pocket of the dress she wore under a "waterproof." You can guess whether she had been wet.

Incidentally, I do not consider the view from Nevis by any means equal to that from many slightly lower Scottish tops.

The first part of the path is rather like the bed of a burn. This is the stretch mounting along the flank of that outrider of the Ben called Meall an t' Suidhe, and pronounced approximately Meal an Too-i. Just at the back of this is a lochan, in which there are trout, and you are free to make surmises as to the explanation of their presence. This lochan the trail leaves on its left, to curve round and cross the Red Burn by a wooden bridge. Beyond that is the real Ben. Once upon a time you could take a sheltered breather in a hut known as the Halfway House, doubtless a relic of Observatory Days, but time, weather and fuel-hunters made away with it at last, and probably you will not now notice even its site. As regards elevation, half of your heavy task may be done, but before you see the big, flat-topped cairn, you will possibly have decided that the second half, with its bleak, dry, stony zig-zags is not only longer than the first but interminable.

As you slog up that path, do not allow concentration on your final objective to monopolise all your thoughts. Look about you as you walk, for on every side there is something to see. Sometimes the unexpected rewards you. My best sight of a buzzard was awarded me below the Halfway point : I heard the bird screaming—nearer and nearer—and suddenly it swept out of the cloud in front of me, and was not many yards away when, startled to an extra outcry, it banked and swooped away.

The summit, for that of Scotland's highest mountain, is disappointing, being a great plateau of boulders. Do not, however, imagine that you have seen the real Ben Nevis because you have strolled round that plateau and have also gazed at the mountain from some point on road or railway whence it appears just an elephantine lump. Taking due care, approach the north-eastern edge of the plateau ; look down some of the gullies, such as the famous Gardiloo, and you may well shrink back. Your gaze drops into a gulf. That is the side of the mountain which draws the real climbers. The " hut " of the Scottish Mountaineering Club is down there, a solid stone building with every convenience and even some luxuries. It stands beside the wild burn known as the Allt a Mhuillin (pronounced Voolin), which rises between the Ben and its neighbour Carn Mhor Dearg (Jerrag). Around Nevis there are two Carn Deargs as well as Carn Mhor Dearg—the big red crag or height— so do not let your map confuse you.

The name Gardiloo relates to the cry of the Edinburgh housewives of old times ; before throwing slops from the high windows of the " lands " they shouted their version of " Gar' de l'eau ! " Down there the Observatory refuse was thrown, and at one time a little wooden " jetty " remained to indicate the dizzy stance of the bucket-emptier.

As you look down that gully, remember that it is amongst the routes of the cragsmen. I once owned a pair of climbing-boots which, one winter day, on the feet of one of my friends, made the descent in circumstances a spectator would have thought were bound to be tragic. The gully was full of snow, the last pitch being icy and perpendicular. Three times, changing places, the two climbers tried to surmount that last obstacle. The lower man had the rope well belayed round his axe, which was driven into the drift up to the head. Twice the leading man slipped, and was held ; the third time he came down straight on to his companion and swept him away, hauling the axe out. Men and axes went shooting down the gully, for something, I suppose, over a thousand feet.

Doubtless the massed snow saved them, but by what miracle did they miss, as they whizzed down, the rocks to right and left ?

My inheritance of those boots was not the direct result of that mishap, I am glad to say. They proved to fit me better than their original owner, that was all ; still, I never donned them without remembering their experience, and wondering whether footgear can carry with them luck, good or evil.

This book leaves real cragsmanship, reverently, alone. The S.M.C. guide to Ben Nevis is the real climber's classic for the mountain. There are many, however, who enjoy a modest scramble, and I must for their sakes indicate one or two in this neighbourhood. By a scramble I mean a really rough, pathless ascent where, at times, hands as well as feet are called into action, and perhaps a little elementary gymnastics are helpful.

If you have a taste for that sort of thing, try climbing Nevis from a certain point near the top of the Glen. Glen Nevis has to be seen, in any case, for its scenery is superb. A car may be taken a long way up it, but when you come to the gorge past Achriach, wheels must be abandoned. The gorge is wild and fine, and after crossing a swing bridge you will be surprised to find yourself in a kind of oasis of level green, with another farm, and the long waterfall of Steall Ban (Ban means " white," by the way) swooping down in your right.

A grand tramp, but a long one, would take you

onwards through really wild country, all the way to
Loch Treig. The route is easier to find and follow
from this end than the other, by the bye starting from
Loch Treig you must con your map carefully, or you
go up the wrong glen. With this Nevis scramble in
your programme, however, stop short of the gorge
where the long water-slide known as Evan's Burn
(Allt Coire Eoghainn) on the map descends on the
left. You cannot possibly miss that landmark, either
in dry weather or wet. It comes down from one of the
Nevis spurs or buttresses. This is one of the Carn
Deargs, not to be confused with Carn Mhor Dearg, to
be visited another time, perhaps. The cascade is your
guide ; follow right up by its side, and eventually you
come to a thoroughly desolate rocky dip. You have
surmounted the buttress, and the rising mass of tumbled
rocks ahead is the upper part of Ben Nevis. Nothing
remains for you to do but to continue scrambling,
taking care how you step on loose stones ; this is no
tourist route, even if not a climb. In cloudy weather
it may well dismay you, for it seems to lead up and up
endlessly into the grey confusion of cloud ; but perseverance will at last surmount it. There are no difficulties, and it really does lead to the summit.

That route is far less boring than the tourist path,
and more interesting in various ways. I once saw a
group of goats on Carn Dearg, led by a magnificent
billy, with grand sweeping horns. It is conjectured
that these goats may be the descendants of escaped
domestic ones, but nothing could be wilder than were
those. Close approach to them was impossible ; without
field-glasses my glimpse would have missed all details.

It seems a duty to repeat, from time to time, the

advice not to go off beaten tracks on the hills without map and compass, and a rough notion as to their use. Cloud may come down and transform even the familiar, and nobody wants to wander bewildered in a stony wilderness, or to have to be looked for.

And let me also deprecate casual scrambles by the inexperienced just anywhere on the " easy " side of Nevis. Some of those slopes are most treacherous, with just a skin of moss, or almost rootless turf, over smooth rock, and some of the slopes which start with an easy gradient steepen rapidly as they rise. The too-enterprising explorer may presently find himself awkwardly placed—unable to get higher, and with no alternative but a really nasty descent. I hate discouraging enterprise, but that mossy stuff, those imitation handholds of grass and heather-tufts, would, I think, be avoided even by the experienced rock-climber. It is neither one thing nor the other.

I had my lesson on the face of Meall an t'Suidhe above Achintee. It looks easy from below, but I thoroughly hated it before, thinking myself mighty lucky, I got to the top.

(A digression here—a digression which is also a confession. Now and then, as on that occasion, I talk to myself when beginning to be frightened. Am I the only scrambler who has this habit and finds it helpful? Sometimes a man's nerves tell him he is stuck and cannot possibly get up or down without mishap ; or that he has lost his way in the mist and will never find it, or that the wind and the rain or snow is over-stepping the liberties of rough comradeship. When I am that man, I know that I tell myself not to be a fool ; to weigh up the situation calmly ; and the effect is that reason takes charge again and the possibility of panic fades away. An old proverb says that he who talks to himself talks to the devil; it is the silliest slander on the sort of soliloquy I indulge in and even recommend. If there is somebody with you, his bad moments—like his spells of fatigue—won't coincide with yours, and you can take one another to task; if you are alone, why not listen to your experience and common sense when they are available to silence the gibbering of your weaker instincts?)

Attaining the summit of Nevis by this route you have the satisfaction of having avoided paths. All paths have been made by somebody, and you don't always want to avail yourself of the guidance of predecessors. The grass, rocks or heather before your next step in the right direction is *your* path, and there should be a satisfaction in that fact. Other people, perhaps plenty, climb Ben Nevis that way—I once found a groat half-way up, which proved that mine was not a " first ascent "—but not enough of them to leave a track to make you, in some degree, a sheep.

Unless you want to return to Fort William by the long trail down Nevis, and if you are still feeling pretty good, you can make a most interesting descent over Carn Mhor Dearg, the spur on the eastern side of the Ben. This is a much more definite top than Carn Dearg, and the approach to it involves a rough descent from the summit on to a narrow ridge that sweeps up the sharp top of Carn Mhor Dearg. You will, if you are lucky, find a little cairn on the eastern edge of the Nevis plateau top indicating the best route by which to descend to the start of that ridge. A fine ridge it is, serrated and narrow, and you need not be ashamed if

at one point you choose to proceed in a sitting posture
with one leg hanging down each side . . . . Rock-
climbers will laugh at this ; I repeat that I am addressing
the uninitiate. It simply would not be fair to tell
them that that ridge meant a mere walk. I once heard
a famous climber sniff at Striding Edge, which runs
down from one side of Helvellyn ; he said that " a
rheumatic old woman could go along it on crutches."
Well, so she might, had she been accustomed to it in
her supple youth—and yet I have heard of a lady
fainting on it. On some of its rocks are inscriptions
recording fatalities. And that reminds me of an
occasion long ago when I asked a veteran cragsman
about Crib Goch, a Welsh ridge, as we stood tracing
its dark cockscomb till it merged with the gloomy wet
cloud. " It's *just* a climb," he said. " Don't *pull* the
holds ; press them in. There's nothing in it—still,
we *have* lost a man off it." To me it seemed a very
good scramble, which I might have enjoyed more but
for that needless advice and superfluous information.
Seekers of advice from strangers should remember that
the adviser does not know their standard, and quite
rightly assumes that it is modest.

It is quite possible to dodge the crest altogether,
and make a rough route for yourself along its flanks.
I warn you however that though you thus shirk the
saw-toothed edge, you will give yourself some arduous
work amongst the jumbled slabs and chunks strewn
below. Alone amongst that jumble, one dripping,
sombre day, with the mist cutting off everything beyond
a few yards away I once found myself confronted by
a mass of porphyritic rock, black and shiny in the
wet, shaped exactly like a coffin.

Having reached the tip of Carn Mhor Dearg, you can either descend right ahead and somehow make your way across (or through) the river and so gain the high-road, or you can cut left, cross the Allt a Mhullin and so work back on to the lower part of the Nevis path.

Fort William is the reverse of an attractive town, but as a base for almost every variety of walk and climb it can have few rivals in Britain. Certain hills are apt to monopolize interest of casual visitors to their locality ; Nevis is an outstanding case in point. Yet all around his great bulk are grouped other hills of dignified stature, and full of interest of every kind. Let me suggest another ridge walk, this time without any excuse for the straddling business. It starts from near the head of the glen. Instead of crossing the wooden bridge at Achriach you look to your right, and there stand two fine heights, Sgur a Mhaim (pronounced something like Vuhm or Vöm) and Stob Ban. (Ban means white, by the way ; notice the quartzite rocks at the top). Make your way up either. I say "make your way" because though you may find paths intended for the use of ponies in the stalking season, you will not find one intended as your guide to any summit.

Perhaps, from below, those two look severe for you, but as you proceed you will discover that there are no difficulties except a fairly steep incline. Having reached the top of, I hope, Sgur a Mhaim, you turn your face in the direction of Fort William and proceed to enjoy a magnificent switchback tramp along the top of the western rampart of Glen Nevis.

You will discover that, broadly speaking, all the mountains in the neighbourhood are shaped like breakers rising more or less gently from the west, and tumbling abruptly to the east. Thus the slopes on the western side of your wide ridge are all quite gradual.

You will be impressed by the great scoop of the Mulach nan Coirean as you walk along the edge of a kind of half-basin, and you will appreciate the new realization you get of the bulk of Nevis opposite. If by chance your walk is on a wet day, you may be compensated for lack of sunshine by strange mist formations along his cliffs ; several thin cloud-strata at different levels, for instance.

Before leaving this neighbourhood, I must recommend a walk down the northern side of Loch Linnhe. The road there is much pleasanter and less frequented than that on the southern side. To begin with you must be ferried across. I never think of that transit without smiling to myself at the memory of one occasion when a local man gave me a " lift " in his boat, and gave me also one of the most cunning and roundabout hints that I have ever heard. As we neared the further shore—I working my passage at one oar—he told me, apropos of nothing in particular, how his farmer brother once gave a stranger a lift in the back of his cart, and looking round just before their destination was reached, realized that the ungrateful passenger had slipped over the tail of the cart and made off, rather than pay for his transport. Did my benefactor fear I might dive and swim for it ?

Opposite Fort William is the tiny hamlet of Trislaig, which is as great a contrast to that town as you could find ; nine miles down the loch is Corran. Every step of the way is beautiful and commands constantly-changing prospects, and at Corran you can get the ferry across and catch the steamer for Fort

William. You can also have some very pleasant easy days on the hills above Trislaig, and from their slopes study the Nevis group to your heart's content.

CHAPTER THIRTEEN

BEN VAIR

SPELLED Bheithir on the map, this is really a group, containing a wide glen at the foot of which lies South Ballachulish, so that it obviously calls for an expedition from Fort William. You get a challenging view of it from Onich or Corran, whence its profile is most alluring. It offers a most delightful " horse-shoe " day, and, if visibility is good, one of the tops commands a prospect which, in my experience, is hardly rivalled.

The morning when I set out by steamer from Fort William for my first visit to Ben Vair, was unpromising, with a falling glass, but I trusted my luck and a hunch, and was rewarded.

Cloud was still low on the hills when I disembarked at Ballachulish, but it steadily rose before me as I mounted, and a fine day kept on improving to the climax of one of those heavenly Highland evenings which obliterate many wet memories.

The barometer ? It is almost a matter of principle with me not to see one before setting forth. So often its predictions are falsified by local conditions, or some arbitrary behaviour on the part of the wind.

My chosen route, which proved satisfactory, left the road about a mile east of the hotel. From that point rises the obvious ridge, interestingly rugged, but with no difficulties, running up to the top of Sgurr Dearg (3,362 feet). From this point Sgorr Dhonuill, about a hundred feet less, looks pretty wild, but while walking amongst and above a wilderness of broken crags, you can evade all difficulties. The ridge is still your definite guide, curving round to drop down into thin woods, through which you will find a way straight down to the pier. That, however, is after a longish and pretty rough trudge amongst strewn rocks, heather, moss-hags and many little lochans. Before you descend in earnest you reach the knob called Creag Gorm (2,372 feet). It is from there that I promise you a view you will put high in your list, for it commands vistas up Loch Leven with its grand enclosing heights, the lower end of Glencoe, and Loch Linnhe in both directions.

I should call this a fairly good day's outing, if it is to be thoroughly enjoyed. To the man or woman out of training or in a hurry, the ups and downs of the long ridge might well be something of a grind, and the afforestation of the lower slopes makes their negotiation laborious ; if you are fit, however, and there is no steamer available, you may find yourself sharing the enthusiasm that some have shewn after Ben Vair has been dealt with, and walk back the twelve miles to Fort William—a gorgeous walk on the right kind of evening. On a more recent visit I was rewarded by my best sight of the " Brocken Spectre " of my shadow, cast on the mist below the crags of Sgurr Dearg, and surrounded by a " rainbow " halo. The photograph I tried shows that aura only as a faint white ring of course, but is a souvenir worth having.

CHAPTER FOURTEEN

BEN BUIDHE AND THE EAGLE FALLS

THIS mountain (3,106 feet), is not perhaps one of the most interesting for its own sake, but the approach to it is a most enjoyable walk, and one of the finest panoramas I know in the Highlands is waiting for you if you reach the summit when visibility is good. It stands about four miles due north of the head of Loch Fyne, and the natural route to its foot is first up the little road that runs above the pretty green strath through which winds the River Fyne, past Merk Cottage and on to Inverchorachan.

A careful driver, not too fussy about his car, can mechanize that part of the expedition, but it is rather a pity to do so.

(At Inverchorachan, where my little party was once delightfully entertained to tea, I listened to an argument which might well have filled with despair a student of the Gaelic less pertinacious than my friend who started it by asking the proper pronunication of a certain word. The shepherd hailed from Skye, his wife from Inverness-shire, and the argument that arose between them never reached a satisfactory conclusion. He said the word thus : she said it otherwise, and both knew they were right).

From Inverchorachan the easiest way up the hill is by the side of the burn that comes down just beyond the house. You presently find yourself in a wide amphitheatre, down the steep sides of which tumble five or six small burns to unite and become the one

which has been your guide.   Picking the easiest further
stage, skirt round this hollow and scramble up to the
ridge, attain its ragged crest and follow it up to the
summit.   There are steepish places, and lots of rock of
sound quality, and if you like to exercise a little cragsmanship on a small scale, opportunities are all around—
though not challengingly in your way.

You will be glad when you reach the cairn and take
your first look round, for the view is really superb ;
if you have already been up a number of the mountains
of the West of Scotland you will here enjoy to perfection
the old hand's treat of picking out old friends and
appreciating their looks from a novel angle.   The whole
glorious *massif* of Cruachan is there for admiration, and
the Ben Lui group, also the Arrochar Highlands.   You
should be able to pick out the Paps of Jura, Ben Nevis,
Bidean, Lawers, the tip of Schiehallion, Ben More and
Stobinian, the Perthshire Ben Vorlich, Ben Lomond,
and Dumyat, the rocky height that boldly and suddenly
ends the western end of the Ochils.

I have a note in my " log-book " which mentions
that on the occasion I have in mind we took less than
two hours, going easily, from Inverchorachan to the
summit ; but time really has nothing to do with the
business, and I mention it merely as an indication to
help you to arrange your programme.

Though any day on a hill can be a good one, for
something, Ben Buidhe — pronounced Boo-i — is
such a magnificent stance for a wide view that I
recommend those who have ample opportunities to
keep on climbing it till they arrive at the top to find
visibility a hundred per cent.

Glen Fyne is worth visiting not only as a route to

a hill. A tramp right up it as far at least as the track will take you makes the sort of outing ideal for the day when you want to be amongst the mountains without getting on to the tops of any. There are such days, I assume, in the lives of all of us.

Again, if you want a walk and a scramble, and to see a waterfall not, I think, seen by many, you should explore the gorge of the Eagle Falls, which comes down from the eastern side of Glen Fyne about a couple of miles above the head of the Loch.

We, a party of three of us, were lured thither by an interesting story picked up from a chance acquaintance met at Ardlui. Realizing the kind of people we were, he asked us if we had ever seen the Eagle Falls, and when we confessed that we had never even heard of them, he went on to say that he believed they were well worth visiting not only for their own sake, but because in a cliff in their gorge could be seen iron pegs driven into the rock, serving as steps down to some cavernous hiding-place, doubtless used in the good old times when so many people had reasons for escaping from others. He gave the story a touch of confirmatory detail by saying that a shepherd he knew had seen those pegs from above, but, doubting their reliability, had made no investigation.

This sounded interesting, and when we went, we took a rope. The burn comes down that hillside in a cleft at a steep angle ; then its banks rise into precipitous rocks, covered for the most part with vegetation of all sorts—moss, grass, ferns, heather and small trees.

To follow the grassy brae would have meant that we were all the time leaving the stream further and further below us, so we decided to keep down, right in the bed, and quite an afternoon we had, negotiating the variety of obstacles provided by pools and water-polished rocks of all shapes and sizes. Plenty of gymnastics there, if you want to keep your boots reasonably dry.

Constantly we paused and scanned the rising cliffs above, on both sides, for those rumoured ancient iron pitons, but no sign of them could we see, or of anything else to suggest that others had ever been at the bottom of this gorge before us.

Then at length we came to an obstacle no gymnastics could overcome ; the falls themselves. They came down in a long white horse-tail, with smooth sheer rock each side. (And what a spectacle in a real spate! There would be no scrambling up the burn's bed then, for it must be filled by a terrific, roaring race of foaming waters).

Still no vestige of an ancient iron peg was to be observed by the most careful scrutiny, and we decided that our Ardlui friend, speaking from hearsay, had got the wrong story, or given the wrong location, and put the pretext for this exploration out of our heads. (Some time later we found reason to believe that the tale had its foundation in the discovery of some desperate cragsman's pitons in a cliff miles away from the Eagle Falls).

Just north of us was a little top with the name of Cruach Tuirc, which we wanted to include in our local bag, though it is only 1,745 feet high. Several lochans lie round about it, and such high little pools are always pleasant to visit.

Having no wish to retrace our steps down the

floor of the gully, we thought we would climb out, up
the southern side, where it looked easy enough.

It was, for the first thirty or forty feet, and then
it began to reveal, more and more plainly, the unpleasant
characteristics of all such damp, steep, romantic-
looking rock-slopes. Its angle became steeper, its
vegetation wetter, looser, and more treacherous as
handholds or resting-places for the feet ; also we had
been scrambling up towards our left, thus bringing
ourselves into such a position that we were above
a considerable overhang : no place for a slide.

I don't pretend that I liked it at all or was making
a good show at it, and there came a moment when I
was about to sing out to the man above me that I was
stuck, when he made a remark to me to the same
effect—and he, I may say, is really a climber, and
a determined one with long arms.

Now I have mentioned that we had a rope. So far
we had not used it, and which of us should now be
carrying it but the third man, quite a long way below
me! If two of us were really "rock-fast," unable to
move up or down, it didn't much matter who had the
rope ; the leader recognised this, and in another minute
I heard him make a move and a scramble, and then he
sang out that he was O.K. and had a good stance ;
could the third man chuck an end of the rope up to me,
and could I then chuck it up to him, and everything
would be all right ?

He had moved, it appeared, at some risk, trusting
his weight to a very small rowan sapling at which he made
a tip-toe, finger-tip grab, and which he thought might
hold, as he had thoughtfully experimented with one
like it earlier in the afternoon.

After a few bad throws and bad misses, we got the end of the rope up to him, and after that all was well, and not long afterwards we were eating tinned apricots by the side of the lochan close to rocks at the summit of Cruach Tuirc.

This wasn't really a desperate adventure, but it had a moment or two of real nastiness, with the compensatory exhilaration of relief.

If there was a lesson to be learned from it, perhaps it was that the last man in a scrambling party is not the one who should be carrying the rope.

CHAPTER FIFTEEN

A CAMPSIE OUTING

WITHOUT going far afield, the man resident or sojourning near Glasgow who seeks the refreshment of hill-walking may find satisfaction in an occasional day or half-day on the Campsie Fells. In character they are much like the Ochils, which is natural, in view of their similar volcanic origin ; both consist mostly of easy grass slopes, with here and there expanses of peat-moss, and with also some quite formidable crags of rather unreliable rock. Better still, they are alike in possessing some surprisingly desolate and lonely stretches, in which the solitary explorer can feel quite away from his everyday world.

My favourite Campsie tramp is from the Blane Valley, over Earl's Seat, and down to Fintry, perhaps returning, if latent energy and time suffice, by the road to Lennoxtown.

As a matter of courtesy the permission of the proprietor might be obtained before your expedition sets forth by my route, as it starts by climbing the stone wall, about a mile and a half south-east along the road from Strathblane, and following up the Ballagan Burn. By asking, you will show that you are not the type of out-door enthusiast who cuts down valuable young trees to " drum up," and lights his fire against the trunk of others too large for his little axe. On your left, as you climb the grass brae, is the waterfall known as Ballagan Spout, in impressive rocky surroundings, and, when the burn is in spate, really spectacular.

In the gorge below it the rock-strata are exposed in
section ; amongst geologists they are well-known as the
Ballagan Beds, and you do not have to be a geologist to
think the few minutes wasted which you should spend
noting the number of thin superimposed layers with
their variety of colours.   This is said to be about 200,
" consisting of limestone, sandstone, and marly slate,
capped by massive beds of whitish sandstone and
trap."

Keep following up the burn, but not close to it ;
rather go parallel over the crests, Dumbreck (1,665),
Owsen Hill (say 1,850), and the Little Earl about
the same as Owsen.   These are only the tops of
undulations, with but gentle dips between ; pleasant
going on a dry day.   From the Little Earl, Earl's Seat
stands up with quite an air, but between these two
tops there is a stretch of rough peat-moss, through
which, particularly after wet weather, you will have to
pick your way with judgment unless you are fond of
scrambling up and jumping off peat hags at every few
yards, black-mudded above the ankles.   Should you
want to make this part of the walk longer, you might
cross the Ballagan Burn before reaching the Little Earl,
and head for the knob to the north-west—delightfully-
named Clachertyfarlie Knowes, and Garloch.   Looking
north-west from the latter, you have an interesting
glimpse of the steep frontage with which the Campsies
suddenly drop to the valley, and to reach it you have
to thrust your way through a heathery, wettish area
where, if you like the feeling of solitude, you certainly
will have what you like.

The best thing about Earl's Seat is the view it
provides—a panorama of peaks along the sky-line,

never twice the same. It is worth going there when snow is lying on the high tops and squalls of it are whirling about them, while now and then between the moving grey veils the crags, gleaming white and blue, catch a sudden sun-burst. On such a day, with the sort of wind to produce these effects, you may find the conditions on the Campsies rougher than perhaps you expected.

During the war a concrete pillar was erected in connection with the Ordnance Survey, and it bears the figures 1662. Do not let it cheat you; whatever those numerals represent, the height you have attained is 1,896 feet, and you will imagine it higher, so wide is the prospect.

From the summit of Earl's Seat head roughly north-north-east, for you must not be in that neighbourhood without looking into the two corries scooped out of the Campsies there. The first is striking and worth seeing, but the second has always seemed to me—and to others, I find—quite unexpected, and an even startling feature, reached for the first time. The Corrie of Balglass is like half a bowl, with a radius of nearly half a mile, the other half having been broken away towards the north. It was the steepness of the sides that impressed me when first I found myself on the brink and with my gaze plunging down the curving cliff, not far from sheer for several hundred feet. A hawk, soaring below me in the " bowl " with the sun brightening the colour of his wings, contributed life to the picture, and emphasised the depth of that very sudden drop.

Fintry is now north-east, with some rather wearisome ups and downs before you reach it. I suggest

that instead of making a bee-line, you follow the course
of the Kilewnan Burn and scramble over the top of the
crag called Dunmore. " Dun " indicates the presence
of a fort, and surely you will think old earthworks
obvious ; also the hollow path that winds down is no
roadway of yesterday.

If you have kept your eyes about you on this
route, you should have seen patches of a plant that
must interest others besides the botanist, if only because
of its habitat.   It is the cloudberry or averon.   In early
summer it bears a white flower very like a bramble's,
its leaves resembling those of that plant.   Later it
produces a bramble-like berry, which passes from yellow
to purple, and is edible but without any very definite
taste.   Its name cloudberry it owes to the fact that
south of the Border it is not found below 2000 feet.
Further north it flourishes lower, and even at sea-level.

My favourite time to arrive at Fintry is late
afternoon in summer, when the narrow valley of the
Endrick in which it lies is partly in shadow, and the
smoke from the houses lined amongst trees along the
road is rising quietly up into the sunshine.   The
downward view under such conditions seems to illus-
trate the word " serenity "—and if the walker has
sound hopes of a meal in the village, his mood as he
makes the final descent ought to be in keeping.

By map measurement, this crossing of the hills
represents only about six miles, but with its switchbacks, divergencies, and rough going, such measurement
is fallacious and misleading.

One of my best days on the Campsies was, by the
way, a frosty one when Glasgow was muffled in fog.
Even at Strathblane visibility was limited to the road's

width, but the mist was of the kind that encouraged the hunch that it was but a thin layer between the valley and the sunshine. So it proved to be ; three hundred feet up the slopes I felt the sun's warmth on my back, and then saw my shadow, vaguely, on the dispersing vapour ahead, with a white halo round it. Another hundred feet, and I was under a blazing blue sky. Looking back was like looking over a grey lake, from which here and there an island of high ground stood up ; the flood of mist was lying even over Loch Lomond, and the Ben was just an island with a peak.

Fintry, when I reached it, was free of mist, and not till I came down towards Lennoxtown in the gloaming was I again submerged.

I have mentioned only one walk about the Campsies but there are of course endless possibles. A visit to the Mickle Bin (1,870 feet) is worth while for a different view ; but look at the map—the whole area invites you.

CHAPTER SIXTEEN

BEN LAWERS

LAWERS, despite its stately height of 3,984 feet, is in placid weather rather a "plodder's" mountain, though it has its cliffs which make an amphitheatre at the bottom of which lies Lochan na Chat —with good fish, I'm told. It stands centrally, however, and dominates a vast area of that marvellous county of Perth, and for all sorts of reasons is well worth climbing. Incidentally, it and its neighbours are a favourite hunting-ground for botanists, certain rare sub-alpines making them their habitat. Up there once with one of the fraternity, I was delighted to observe his enthusiasm. He had never been on a hill of that height, but knew what plants ought to be found, and he climbed at a kind of " gardener's crouch," eyes on the ground for tiny treasure, his progress ever and anon interrupted by a yelp of delight over a discovery. He was seeing what he had read about, including, I remember, Britain's smallest tree, the Dwarf Mountain Willow. That hardy pigmy, boldly claimed as a true tree, never raises its head more than two inches from the ground, most of its stem lying horizontal as taught by the winds that rampage over the high places where it chooses to grow. At most seasons of the year you would never notice it amongst the miniature vegetation of the heights, but in autumn its seed vessels, like thistle-down, drift about with every puff of wind. It grows in great quantities on the Cairngorms.

If you want just to get to the top of Ben Lawers,

the simplest plan is to start from Lawers Hotel or thereabouts, and follow a rather hazy track in what is really an extremely easy ascent over grass.

Let me, by way of suggestion, describe how one July day I made Lawers one feature of as satisfying a hill-outing as I ever had. The weather, I may say, indulged me, for, after the morning mist cleared away, the sky was stainless blue till touched by the softening hues of evening.

Well then, Lawers Hotel was the starting-point from which I set out about half-past eight, with the splendour and heat of the cloudless sun already on my shoulders. On such mornings there is a special quality in the silence, as though the strengthening glory of the day held the world in awe. My programme was, for me, an ambitious one ; I aimed at taking in the whole massif, and, frankly, bagging quite a handful of " Munros." This meant that I must start with Meall Gruaidh (3,280 feet), pretty well due north of Lawers village ; as that village stands 700 feet above the sea it gives you a good start. Gruaidh is grass to the summit, and you can take almost a bee-line on the eastern side of the Lawers Burn. Meall Garbh (3,661 feet), is due west of this top, and the ridge or *belach* between them does not dip so much that you lose a lot of height before your second " Munro " is in the bag.

That morning, heavy mist—of the right kind, the kind that goes on lifting as the sun's power increases— concealed the next " hump," which as its name An Stuc implies is a definite nob astride the ridge ; the eastern side is rock-strewn, and, in the gloom of the mist, looked formidably steep. It is nothing of the kind, and yielded easily to a scrambler's approach. The mist

was dispersing rapidly, and by the time I had surmounted An Stuc, Ben Lawers itself, with the quite
impressive rocky cup holding the lochan, was perfectly
clear.

What a view ! I will just mention that it included
Dumgoyne, that bold knob at the end of the Campsies—
a nob, by the way, which is a perfectly astonishing
view-point.

My next objective was Ben Glas, southwards.
Another Munro—3,085 feet ; and then I turned north-
east across a wide ridge separating watercourses
running north and south, and took in Meall Corranaich
(3,250 feet). A more determined peak-bagger would
have gone on in the same direction and captured Meall
Coire a Leith, another top over 3,000, but I foresaw
that my programme was going to be enough for me.
What I did was to go down towards the north end of
Lochan na Lairige, cross the road that climbs across
from Loch Tay to Glen Lyon, and trudge up to Meall
nan Tarmachan (3,421 feet).

Meanwhile the sun blazed, still high, but despite
my exertions I was not over-warm ; on such occasions
I find that one gets very hot for a short time, and then
forgets about it, as though acclimatised. I was in
shorts, ideal wear for that sort of weather and that sort
of walking. Tarmachan has an interesting, rocky ridge
for a summit. By this time I was looking forward to
easy going, and this part of the itinerary is the roughest
and noblest. It was, in a sense, the climax ; having
at last left it behind me, all that remained was a steady
descent over the hummock of Creag na Caillich (2990 ft.),
aiming for the Bridge of Lochay.

The bracken-thickets on the lower slopes were just

at the height of their strength, making a jungle full of trip-wires, and I was definitely glad when at last I reached the high road with a prospect of being presently horizontal for a spell and relaxing my legs. Enquiries for a billet in Killin met, at first, with failure, but at length I was promised a couch in the sitting-room of a boarding-house ; there I had a bath and a royal meal, which so refreshed me that I joined in a delightful after-dinner stroll.

The couch proved a hard one, but a dear old lady, aware of my nocturnal prospects, spared a pillow from her own bed. With what a glorious day added to my mountain memories I stretched myself out—a day in retrospect all glowing blue and gold, as if it had been spent remote from the real earth, actually in the sky itself.

CHAPTER SEVENTEEN

BEN LUI

IN a company of lovers of this country's high places, a thoroughly satisfying controversy can be started anywhere and at any time by somebody's championship of some mountain as Scotland's most beautiful. Such a claim, and the discussion it initiates, is of course absurd, because the debaters' ideas of what constitutes beauty in a hill all differ, and a single special experience may create an impression which nothing can modify.

On such occasions I enter the lists on behalf of Ben Lui. If hills have personalties—and experience amongst them will persuade you to the superstition that they have—Ben Lui's is genial and friendly where I at least am concerned. I love its general shape, as seen from the north, and its details are as satisfactory. This does not mean that it cannot look grim and even savage, but I have never happened to pay a visit when it seemed also completely hostile. Nevertheless my first ascent, a solitary one, was on a day when its upper half was lost in mist: my second, likewise unaccompanied on a day still worse, with steady rain and plenty of wind into the bargain.

The easiest way up Lui is from the west, or from a point a couple of miles or so along the road from Tyndrum to Dalmally, but the really interesting route, the one which, an ignorant explorer, I took that first day, is up the Central Gully, facing roughly north. The approach is a five mile walk along a rough little track up Coninish Glen, past Coninish Farm. By the time you reach the farm you can really see your mountain, or as much of it as is below the clouds, and I must admit that it may strike you as presenting a certain—shall I say "hauteur" of aspect? With bold rocky buttresses on each side, the hollow side of the mountain rises and narrows, like a great grey fan of scree, with various "fingers" of rock reaching down from the challenging battlement of surmounting crags. A little bridge takes you across the burn on to the mountain itself, and you begin your climb amongst boulders and long tufty grass. Following up the burn, or near it, you can't go wrong, no matter how obscure the upper heights.

Perhaps had those craggy battlements been visible I should have funked that approach; I have been glad ever since that I just went on and on and up and up, on scree growing ever steeper, though of a consistency that made it easy, until I was right up at the rocks and found no difficulty in wriggling a way between them. I don't think mountaineers would call it a climb, but in fairness I report that some scramblers do. I emerged close under the main cairn, which is the most easterly—and on my second visit had such a reception from sheets of rain, flung almost horizontal against the summit ridge, that I might almost have been on a reef within easy spray-reach of a breaking sea. I stayed there only, that time, long enough to appreciate my triumph and to pick up an odd souvenir—a lady's old glove, one of those elbow-length kid ones once worn at dances. (I have never been able to find an altogether satisfactory guess at the reason of its presence there; and what brought a parrot's cage in the middle of the Coolins in Skye, where climbers once found one?) One of the memorable sights of that day was provided by the mist, as, emerging from the clouds, I looked down. Caught by wind eddies, wreaths of it were whirling in spirals, like wheels on their rims, the axis of the spirals horizontal.

On a properly wet day, when the burn that has some claims to be regarded as the infant Tay is springing from a source not far from the top of the gully, that long scree is delightful to descend. You can put your heels in and plunge forward at a great rate. Incidentally a great deal of parsley fern grows amongst the stones.

About scree. It varies greatly, and some is most unpleasant, such as the white cape of it on Ben Eighe, of which I shall speak elsewhere. Other varieties tempt you to rush and go flying down, perhaps accompanied by your own little avalanche. This is all very fine and most exhilarating, but don't be too reckless. To attempt to walk carefully down loose scree, stepping gingerly from stone to stone, is no use ; on the other hand—well, an experienced Lakeland cragsman made to me the comment that he had seen too many scree-flyers brought home on shutters. He was hinting at the possibility of some solid projection amongst the loose stuff, and a sudden somersault. Moderation is the wise policy in this as in most things.

I fancy that, if, having climbed Lui for your first time from the back, you were invited to descend through that fringe of rock and down the scree, you might hesitate, particularly on a day when it appeared to plunge into a grey vacuity ; having come up it, you would, I think, share my feeling that it is one of those places which gives you the pleasant illusion of being tough while actually it isn't anything of the sort.

I still remember my feelings of triumph as I tramped splashing back to Tyndrum, with Coninish Glen full of racing waters.

I have mentioned parsley fern as finding a congenial habitat on the Lui rocks ; another interesting plant is the *rosea rhodiola*, a stonecrop known as roseroot or midsummer-men.   Dry a piece of the root and it smells faintly like a rose ; that explains one name.   The other is queerer.   It certainly puts forth its turret of yellow flowers above the spire of glaucous leaves about midsummer ; but not till I read Kilvert's Diary did I get an inkling of the reason for the other.   Kilvert, writing of country customs in a county on the Welsh border, refers to the plant as one used by girls for the same kind of romantic divination as was practised at Hallowe'en, to enable them to secure a vision of their future husbands.   Regarding its occult properties I am ignorant, but I can answer for its astonishing vitality.   A scrap of the root, hung from a nail on a bedroom wall, put out little leaves for two years before finally abandoning the struggle.   Removed from its moist heights, it survives and flourishes and endures endless transplantings ; a most accommodating flower. Like the thrift or sea-pink, its favourite habitats are the high mountains and the sea-shore.

This botanical digression having been started, let me add to it by remarking on the additional pleasure to be had from mountain-scrambling by even the most superficial knowledge of the appropriate flora.   Many of the true mountain plants are naturally brilliant, and they borrow additional vividness from the contrast with their surroundings.   To see a patch of purple saxifrage glowing through the mist, within a few feet of the edge of a snowdrift and close by a curtain of eight-foot icicles, as I have done, is in its way as memorable as to see whole snow-clad mountain-mass flush rosy at dawn.

For the collector of specimens, may I suggest that an excellent container is a sponge-bag hung from a jacket-button. It keeps the plants or mosses moist, and the bearer undamped from their proximity.

Mountaineers consider that the right time to climb Lui by that gully is when it is snow-packed. It offers over a thousand feet, with, sometimes, a cornice to cut through at the top.

One early spring day, with a friend from the south who had never walked on " real " snow before, I tramped up Coninish Glen, hoping to introduce him to the mountain, but doubtful of being able to do so, for various reasons. One of them was the fact that the gully was snow-filled, another that he was wearing shoes, and a third that we had only one ice-axe between us, and no rope.

We started up towards the gully and the lowering cloud, however, and found footprints, obviously recent. Better still, we found a beautiful ladder of steps cut for us. This was too tempting, and, perhaps foolishly, we carried on, full of gratitude to those who had done the work. On that occasion that work cannot have been very hard, for the surface of the snow was softish and cutting would not be the chipping business which it sometimes is.

Not far below the summit-ridge we met our benefactors returning, a fully equipped and roped party, who looked at us rather sideways, as though

they would like to have snubbed us for being what the
Army calls " improperly dressed."

As the man who had been there before, I led with
the axe, and presently surmounted in triumph the last
few feet of almost perpendicular beaten snow. Then
I turned and looked down at my friend, and a very
strange spectacle he offered. He was represented by
little more than his hat, his shoulders and his up-
stretched arms, his background being the wan nothing-
ness of snow merging into mist.

He declined the offer of a helping hand from above,
saying " I want to do this myself ; " but next moment
changed his mind and invited it, the reason being that
one of his footholds had given way, the snow, as I have
said, not being really firm.

I thought that ascent a pretty good apprenticeship, not foreseeing what a fine climber that novice
was to become.

Deciding not to return by the same way, we made
for the ridge and shoulder curving westwards, and made
a mistake that has been made there before and since
under the same misty conditions ; we were misled by
the ground into going too far west, and giving ourselves
a far longer walk than was necessary before regaining
the path that runs past Coninish Farm. The tendency
is to avoid too widely the cornices and slopes that
edge the crest on the right, and so to miss the more
direct downward-sloping shoulder.

The gully ascent can be considerably varied by
choosing routes between different rock " fingers."

The most beautiful winter view of Lui which I
have ever had was one April morning after snow had
been falling. Light cloud was low, but ever and anon

it brightened so that we saw " the sun with pale face wading through the mist," and suddenly, just before we reached Coninish Farm, it was blown clear from the Ben, and there soared the mountain, all dazzling white snow and blue shadow, with the azure sky behind, a glorious and unforgettable vision. It lasted no more than ten minutes, and for the rest of the day we moved through wet mist, though in the left branch of the gulley which we chose the snow-surface was firm, and the rocks about the summit were slippery with plates of ice.

The following afternoon is memorable to us both because we were to all intents and purposes blown off a neighbouring hill, Ben Odhar, which rises just to the north of Tyndrum railway station. A strong north-easter was blowing the snow in scurries across the long wide ridge, but we thought a trudge up there would be a pleasant Sunday afternoon breather after our rather strenuous Lui expedition on the Saturday.

We both wore balaclavas and a reasonable amount of clothing, but soon realised that we had been frivolous in our preparations. Thanks to the direction of the wind, the snow was drifting deep and soft on each side of the ridge, so that we were compelled to walk along the top, the wide "spine," where we got the full force of the bitterly cold gusts with their whirling particles.

It seemed to me that that day the wind was piercing not merely my clothing, but getting through my skin and rattling the bones within. Not only was it shark-toothed ; that wind was also a heavy-weight, and resisted our every step with punches that kept us staggering without an instant's respite ; and every yard of the way was going to get worse than its predecessor—the dizzy spin of the snow-spray across the climbing ridge proved that most graphically.

Talking was of course impossible, but presently my friend, a much tougher individual than I claim to be, bellowed in my ear as a furious thrust of the gale flung us together, " Aren't we mugs for going on ? " I answered by a smart left wheel, and in another moment we were plunging through the leeward drift towards the sheltered slopes. As always on such occasions of defeat, we soon began to think we had been soft to retire—but that mood sets in when the body has reduced its protests; still, I wish we had each had the extra cardigan that would have made all the difference.

A longish walk in the neighbourhood of Lui, highly to be recommended, is that from the summit—however you elect to get there, over Ben Oss (3,374 feet), and Ben Dubhcraigh (3,204 feet), and on till you strike the Glen Falloch road. As Lui is 3,708 feet, you would " bag " three Munros for your trouble, and the descent between each top is not considerable. I could imagine that in thick or wild weather some careful watching of the route would be necessary, but Loch Oss, to be passed on your right as you follow the high ground in a curve on to Dubhcraigh, is a useful land-mark—not to be confused with the lochan on Dubh-craigh itself, however. My experience of that walk was on as glorious a day as ever blesses the Highlands, and that is saying something.

Even as we sat on the top of Lui to cool, the air was motionless, save for a strange miniature whirlwind that for a few seconds set scraps of dried grass spinning a few feet off the ground.

From the top of Dubhcraigh we made for Allt

Fionn Ghleanne—the burn in little Glen Fion. It is a
beautiful, typical West Highland mountain stream, with
some pools that day were so tempting that we stripped
and went into one long enough to allow a few swimming
strokes. We bathed not only for refreshing, but in the
hope of a brief respite from the clegs. They certainly
did not submerge and attack under water, but they
were ready for any exposed area of skin. I have a
photograph of one member of the party swimming
with his hat on. As we trudged down Glen Falloch
that evening, stewed with heat, we were overtaken by
a baker's van and given a lift. The interior was full
of bread and bannocks and such ; there was no room
for passengers beside the driver, and so we sat on the
top. Its surface, as is the way with such vehicles, was
slightly cambered ; the van bounced and swayed
wildly ; overhanging branches thrashed at us as we
swept along, and the rail round the top was only an
inch or two high and gave little but moral support.
Still, we descended for a meal at Ardlui with a feeling
of survival and of triumph to which that last few miles
of pitch-and-toss no doubt contributed.

CHAPTER EIGHTEEN

BEN CRUACHAN

WERE not Ben Lui my favourite Scottish mountain, Cruachan would be. The whole mass of it, with its array of superb tops, achieves the marvel of living up to the glorious sound of its name. Yet I am assured that name means, probably, just " a great heap."

To attempt to deal with the group, for Cruachan is that, of course, in a few pages is a sort of sacrilege, and yet sometimes a little lyric says more than an elaborated epic.

Standing so near the Atlantic, Cruachan is often cloud-wrapped and rain-swept, but if you visit its tops often enough, fate will some time smile on your persistence, and give you such a day of splendour as was one of mine. That was not my introduction, however ; it has seemed my luck, when making my first pilgrimage alone to any hill, to be treated coldly or roughly.

The Taynuilt end of the massif is the one from which to start, whether you intend to do only the two main tops or to make the complete traverse of all of them. The day when I introduced myself was as wet a day as even the West Highlands can produce, but, as usual, defiance of the rain had its peculiar rewards.

Leaving Taynuilt, you have a mile and a half of highroad to trudge, then you cross the Bridge of Awe, and there before you are the slopes you have to tackle. For me, that day, they rose into grey soaking cloud, drifting low ; and, since the month was July, the bracken was in places shoulder-high, so that long before reaching the open braes I was wet enough not to worry any more. I reached the peak, but to this day do not know exactly how ; that is to say, I have never in clear weather been able to trace the route by which I did so ; I must have worked round to the north side, bewildered by the wet obscurity, for my last couple of hundred feet was up a steep mass of jumbled boulders, quite a little scramble, which does not exist on the orthodox route. What contributes to the undoubted satisfaction, exhilaration, of standing, alone and rain-soaked and wind-whipped, on a mass of rocks islanded amongst grey, wet cloud-wreaths, three thousand feet and more above sea-level ? Self-approval at having got there is one ingredient, but not, I am sure, the chief ; probably none of us can explain. In any case I was thoroughly happy, as I have so often and so gratefully been in similar circumstances.

My plan was to cut down and ultimately reach Loch Awe station. Roughly, the direction was obvious despite the limitation of visibility, for everywhere water was going my way. I do not think I have ever seen a more watery mountain-side than Cruachan's that day ; every little burn was raging and racing, and between their channels the water was sliding in clear sheets across the moss and grass. Descending that long slope was like taking part in an excited and hurrying procession ; I went splashing down aquatically escorted.

The final descent to the road is precipitous in some places, but it is always possible to move along and select a negotiable drop.

That was my introduction ; other visits to Cruachan

have been favoured by weather memorable for other reasons.

One other summer morning, starting betimes, I was standing on the edge of the cliffs overlooking Glen Etive while the sun, not yet high, was dispersing the vapoury haze below and around me, and there, on the pale wisps drifting above the glen, I saw my shadow surrounded by a rainbow ring—a small example of the Brocken Spectre. (In his book *With Rope and Rucksack in the Scottish Highlands*, Dr. Baker mentions seeing this phenomenon from the same position.)

My best Cruachan day of all was with a friend, starting at Taynuilt and finishing at Dalmally—or rather at the Dalmally end of the foot of the slopes of Monadh Driseig, where his wife welcomed us with tea and transport. Everything was that day as nearly perfect as a day on earth could be. Visibility might have been better, to be sure, but the haze that veiled far distances was the kind that so often accompanies settled fine weather, and nobody worthy of Cruachan could have complained.

The sun shone for us from dawn till dusk, through one of those days which seem to pay for all the wet and mist and cold that we learn to take philosophically and pretend to like. The tops we traversed were the " Taynuilt Peak " (3,611 feet), Cruachan's true top, (3,689 feet), Drochaid Glas (3,312 feet) ; Stob Garbh (3,215 feet), and Beinn a Bhuirdh (2,936 feet). This may read like a formidable list, but the performance involves less climbing than the heights suggest, the drops between them being of no great consequence. This tramp from crest to crest of Cruachan is perhaps the best ridge-ramble I know ; the first part is particu-

R.K.H.

BEN CRUACHAN, FROM DUNSTAFFNAGE

larly fine, partly rocky underfoot, with crags dropping into Glen Noe on the north, while the view along Loch Awe towards sunset, from the descending slopes of Beinn a Bhuirdh, was that day quite beyond description for its great glow of light upon the gleaming waters and the many-coloured woods and braes and crags.

This is a good long day's excursion, and the enthusiast may make it still longer by taking in a top or two we missed.

The group is of inexhaustible interest. There are rock-climbs upon it, though perhaps not many for the ambitious, but in the right kind of winter or spring weather it has everything that the snow and ice-lover can wish for.

The visual memory seems to collect, from the impressions of a special day, one or two pictures which, in the course of time, become representative of the whole experience. My first ascent of Cruachan leaves me as its "illustrations" the picture of the dark jumble of great wet boulders above me, rising dimmer and dimmer into the grey drive of the cloud and rain in which at last I found the cairn ; the glass-like sheen of water flowing over the moss and grass of the southern slopes, and the dark spires of tree-tops above the loom of the Pass of Brander, marking the broken line of cliff through which the wildly-careering burns made their final plunge off the mountain.

My memories of the visit described above gather round very different pictures ; first, the steep lower slopes, thinly treed, where amidst the brittle, rustling, bleached relics of last year's bracken were thrusting up the spring shoots like little green croziers, with here and there primroses and dog-violets for company ;

then the rocks high up along the ridge between the two main summits, warm and warm-toned in the glorious sunlight, with patches of hard snow all a-sparkle ; the shadowed white-streaked gullies plunging down from the ridge's northern side, and the blue of tiny lochans on the sunny southern flanks. The limited visibility served to accentuate that precious feeling of remoteness from the bothers of everyday life. In that serenity nothing seemed to move all day but ourselves and the sun, he towards the zenith and then the west, we from top to top eastwards.

From the airy, magnificent spaciousness of such a day you return with a sense of gratitude of which something surely remains long after the purely physical exhilaration has subsided.

CHAPTER NINETEEN

GLEN TURRET AND BEN CHONZIE

AFTER having observed Ben y Hone, or Ben Chonzie, many a time, something of a lump, from the Ochil tops serving chiefly as a mark on the line for the Lawers group, I was glad when an opportunity came to walk over it. Though 3048 feet in height, it is not an outstandingly interesting hill, but the seven-mile walk towards it up Glen Turret, from Crieff, however, is quite worth while, and as nobody wants to retrace his footsteps, the rambler who has gone up Glen Turret might as well go down into Comrie by the Lurg Burn. And to reach the Lurg Burn his most interesting way is over Ben Chonzie, sometimes called Ben y Hone.

This is a walk which demands a sunny day, with good visibility, for the immediate surroundings are inclined to be tame. (Saying so, I reveal an individual prejudice, I suppose ; I prefer my mountain scenery rough). No difficulty presents itself with regard to the route. A real road runs up Glen Turret as far as Glenturret Lodge at the head of the Loch of the same name ; thence the burn is your guide to tiny Lochain Uaine, having reached which you are already 1,523 feet above sea-level, for the expenditure of little climbing energy. Anywhere by Lochan Uaine will do for your starting-point for the hill itself. It commands a grand view, and that is perhaps the best that can be said for Ben y Hone.

Having absorbed the prospect to your heart's content, you can either drop down due east until you strike a track that runs from Glen Almond to Comrie, developing to the rough road down Glen Lednock, some four miles above that little town, or you can do as we did on the occasion I have in mind, and make a line practically due south across broken country, taking burns and what not in your stride, and getting into Glen Lednock that way. A track starts at the farm of Carroglen and, after about three miles, joins the main road under a mile east of Comrie.

My retrospect of my only visit to Ben y Hone is coloured by the weather, which was typical of April in a shrewish mood, grey, with a wind which, on the high ground, kept us hurrying. We were both lightly clad, and I think we made that bee-line across country as much to get out of the wind, and warmed up, as because we were in a hurry to be home.

Of course for anyone at all that round I have described makes a delightful and not too strenuous walk ; I am particularly glad to have done it because, ever since, I can con that piece of country—the steep-sided V of Glen Turret, and the mound of Ben Chonzie, from the Ochil tops, without being worried by ignorance of what they are like at close quarters.

CHAPTER TWENTY

THE GOATFELL HORSE-SHOE

ARRAN, of course, requires a book to itself. What an island ! What a playground, within an hour or two of a great city ! Its walks are inexhaustible and of every character except the dull. The one I best remember I am tempted to say cannot be beaten on the island, but the statement would be open to challenge by plenty of enthusiasts. I daresay my judgment is coloured by the fact that that ramble and scramble is associated with the best of weather, and the best of company.

Our " base " was Corrie. From there we made our way along the coast road to Sannox, and started our upward journey by getting on to Suidhe Phairghais (Sui Fergus), which is almost 1,800 feet high ; till evening we seldom dropped much below that pleasant height. The distant prospects were not good, but the haze that veiled them was of the compensatory kind that is the surety for a great day of warmth and sunshine. The Peak of the Castles (Caisteal Abheal), 2,725 feet, was our next objective. The ridge leading to it is as interesting as you like to make it, with great heaps of rough granite scattered all about, challenging you to test your clambering skill by " bouldering "—and what daring feats one tackles when the danger is of a drop of only a few feet ! The ridge's great feature is one that figures in about fifty per cent. of the paintings of Arran, that great V-shaped cut, like a cleft made by an axe-blow, called Ceum na Caillich, the Old Woman's

I

Leap, or the Carlin's Step. At a distance, and against the sky, it looks formidable ; so it does, slightly, when you arrive at it in your progress up the ridge. Do not be bluffed, however ; take that cool second look, and you will notice that the lie of the rocks makes it easy for you.

At one point, admittedly, there is a rock mass which seems to push you uncomfortably near the brink of a rather long drop ; it overhangs the sloping boulder down which you wriggle, leaving just enough room for your body—only just enough ; if you timidly squeeze in as far as possible from that edge, you may, particularly if bulky, find yourself jammed. (I have found a button lying near, a trophy torn by the mountain from some over-squeezed wriggler). The fact is, however, that there is no need at all to shrink far from the edge ; the rock is so rough that the friction of your clothes is a perfect safeguard. The same bit of scrambling on a mountain different geologically would be quite tricky ; you would be sliding instead of wriggling.

When you have got to the bottom and started the simpler scramble up the opposite side and look back, you will, if not a climber, be quite pleased with yourself to see what you have done, and will want to do it again.

Plenty more opportunities for bouldering await you on the rest of the ridge, for the granite slabs are piled on one another—samples of what is called the Cyclopean Wall on Goatfell. These gymnastics can, however, all be avoided if they are not to your taste.

The ridge continues interesting all the way to the summit of Cir Mhor (pronounced Cir Vore), which is 2706 feet high, and as rugged a mountain as any in Scotland. Though you can walk up it, you are surrounded by really tough climbs, on which the cragsmen are thoroughly satisfied to exercise themselves. To me the Cir Mhor slabs always wear a specially forbidding aspect, particularly when dark and gleaming with wet.

Between this top and Goatfell the ground drops fairly steeply, and you have quite a strenuous ascent to face before reaching the top of Goatfell, but it is a much more interesting and less-used way than that from Brodick, which is marked by a path, and is a regular "tourist route." From Goatfell we turned our footsteps north, with another delightful ridge, this time heathery, running right along to Am Binnein and Cioch na h Oighe, the latter a rather surprising summit, the drop from which down towards Sannox is as steep a heather-and-boulder brae as I know.

The day our party descended everything was so dry that to make the best of the declivity we sat and tried to slide. Just before reaching the point where the slope eases off into the valley, one of the party discovered that, his camera-case having been unfastened, a valuable lense had escaped. Of course we climbed back and looked for it, and to our great surprise found it, so that apparently the hay-stack does sometimes surrender the needle.

On such a day as was granted us, that horse-shoe itinerary makes as fine a rough ridge walk as you will find anywhere, with the Carlin's Step as its high spot. If you think, having inspected it, that you do not fancy that wriggle down you can dodge it, and by-pass by scrambling along the side of the ridge below.

I have praised the helpful roughness of the Arran granite, but I ought also to point out that in some places it disintegrates in a curious way, and can be treacherous. Two of us were once having some mild fun with a rope in the Devil's Punch-bowl, when my friend sang out to me to watch when he gave a shove to the sturdy-looking pillar of rock round which he had been about to belay. It wobbled, and I think he could have pushed it over. Around the Punchbowl a good deal of the rock seems to be rotten like that piece ; so care is needed even for the scrambler.

ON THE WITCH'S STEP

W.K.H.

CHAPTER TWENTY-ONE

SOME WALKS AROUND CRAWFORD

SOME of us make the great mistake of thinking that the walks, whether valley-walks or hill-walks, which we know best are inevitably the best there are. I am one of those whose natural inclination, when a holiday in Scotland is in sight, is to react to the prospect after the manner of the compass needle, and turn to the north. Every time, for whatever reason, I have not followed that instinct, but made a pedestrian raid in some other direction, I have been glad, having made discoveries which explained the enthusiasm of other men for other points of the compass.

This is not to say that my allegiance to the Scottish north-western Highlands has been in any way weakened, or my views altered as to what is the best part of Scotland.

A short stay at Crawford, in Upper Clydesdale, opened my eyes to the fact that there are miles upon miles of high grassy country, not far away, which is ideal country for wandering—glorious terrain for the fell-walker. Tinto Hill I had known of old—not a particularly inspiring hill, but, once more, worth walking up for the view. I have seen Tinto, on a specially clear day when Glasgow was for some reason less smoky than usual—perhaps during the serenity of the July Fair Holidays—from high ground west of the city. But it has not in my experience been possible to indentify that view-point from " Tinto Tap.")

I suggest as a typical day from Crawford a switch-

back round two of us did once on a showery July day.
It measures on the map about twelve miles, if flat
straight measurement means anything on a piece of
country so undulating. Setting out northwards we
made for Tewsgill Hill (1,867 feet), crossed its summit,
and went on to Rome Hill (1,852 feet), with no great
depression to cross between the two. From Rome Hill
we turned south-east, and down hill, crossed the Camps
Water and walked to the top of Yearngill Head (1,800
feet). We had planned to go further, but very heavy
rain came on and we were not in one of our tough moods,
so, after being delightfully entertained to tea at Hare-
cleuch Farm, we ingloriously took the track straight
down the Midlock Water back into Crawford.

Another day we began by taking the train to
Elvanfoot Station, changing there, and then taking
another to Wanlockhead—which nobody can now do,
since that most fascinating little line meandering
through the hills is out of commission. From Wanlockhead we climbed Lowther Hill (2,377 feet), and then
cut across country to the Dalveen Pass, down that,
and made a diversion which brought us to Durisdeer,
where we basked in a field till came the 'bus which took
us lazily back. These two walks can be thus easily
and briefly summarised, but that by no means indicates
that they were lacking in detailed interest. They
kept us on high ground all the time ; Crawford itself
is more than six hundred feet above sea-level. Then,
though these hills are almost all grassy, with little rock
exposed anywhere, they have some of the steepest
grass braes I know, and if you conscientiously follow
the straight route—as from Lowther Hill to the Dalveen
Pass, which is a most romantic-looking cleft for part

of its length—you will encounter a great variety of leg-work. That interesting plant, the cloudberry, described elsewhere in these pages, caught our attention on some of the higher ground. It was on one of those walks that for the only time in my life I held in my hands a half-grown curlew chick. It had out-grown its nestling fluffiness, but had not yet achieved the graceful form of the adult whaup; a kind of hobbledehoy of a bird, most strongly suggestive of an ostrich when, released, it sprinted off, not, I think, desperately alarmed by its experience.

CHAPTER TWENTY-TWO

ARGYLL'S BEN VORLICH

TWO Ben Vorlichs compete in popularity. Both are glorious mountains. The one I write of now is the one for which I have always started from Ardlui. You get on to the hill easily, passing under the railway close to the station. Look at your map and compare it with the ground, and you will see that to the north a shoulder curves round towards the summit. That ought to suggest itself to you as the obvious route. That ridge is called on the map Stob na Coinnich Bhacain. It forms one side of a wide, boulder-strewn, thinly wooded corrie or glen, down which runs a burn. You could of course follow that burn up to a high point on the Ben's shoulder, but my advice is almost always to choose ridges. On them you avoid a lot of sloppy going, you see wide views all the time, and you are not constantly compelled to make detours. The ridge mentioned will lead you, not perhaps gently, but honestly, to a point from which, in clear weather, the rest of the route is obvious. If cloud is down, nothing is obvious except the necessity for a compass. Vorlich has two cairns, not very far apart, and on my first misty visit I should never have known of the slightly higher one, at 3092 ft., but for a sudden break.

It is a rugged hill, and its various ridges can be puzzling. One day when everything was wrapt in motionless white mist and snow lay deep, my companion and I felt as though we were tramping in " the country beyond the world's end " ; only the black projecting fang of a rock here and there reassured us of the earth's solidity ; the junction of mist and cornice-edge was almost impossible to locate. The other man was an enthusiastic compass expert, and I wisely left the navigation to him. In spite of his skill we must have been a few degrees out in our readings, with a result that we made our descent a good deal further down the Loch than we intended. That day, as we approached the road, I saw something which halted me and made me sing out to my friend to look and see if he saw what I did. Far above where I had been peering in the hope of seeing the loom of the heights on the opposite side of the Loch there loomed a vague and awesome mass, like some menacing mountain in a nightmare. It was what I was hoping to see, but we were very much nearer the lochside road, and those opposite heights, than we imagined, and the mist had played one of its typical and eerie tricks upon us. (I have never forgotten how, a novice wandering more or less astray in an attempt to reach Ben Ime in dense wet cloud, I suddenly saw, as if it were moving towards me and about to topple over, a mighty black spire of rock where, an instant before, had been only the drifting raincloud. It was the north peak of the Cobbler, but by no means that peak as sunshine shows it. Tearing out of that grey blur of cloud it was a feature from a Doré landscape, something that made the hair stir on my scalp despite my gratitude for its revelation as a landmark. A sheep in mist can look like a mastodon ; what may not a crag suggest ?)

One of my best days on Ben Vorlich was in November. Two of us motored up to Ardlui, and I wish that the many who know Loch Lomond only in the summer might have seen it as we saw it. The woods and hills were superb in rich colours, brightening and dimming as the racing clouds trailed their shadows over them ; the dark, grey-blue water was alive with leaping white horses, lashed by a furious northerly wind, and above all soared the tops, pure white.

Some of the Highland hills do not live up to the suggestion of their glorious names. (I am not sure that Schiehallion does ; but as that is a hill of the Good Folk, I had better be careful what I say. As it is, I have encountered on its tip, sunshine, hail, and thunder all within ten minutes). Both the Vorlichs emphatically do—and this one never more triumphantly in my experience than that day.

After the October rains the lower slopes were soaking, and every burn white and noisy. To our pleasant surprise we were sheltered from the wind as we trudged past the little farm of Garristuck, and worked along the grassy, boulder-dotted slopes beneath the crags of Stob na Coinnich Bhacain.

From there, such glimpses as we caught of the true top, appearing now and then dark and jagged through the grey cloud, looked remote and even forbidding. Strangers to the hill might well, seeing the summit from that point, decide that Ben Vorlich was a " whole-day hill," but we had only four hours of an early-darkening afternoon, and found it ample. The wide and lovely Coire Creagach, with its torrent and its sparse trees, clasped between Vorlich's two easterly ridges, had that afternoon its appropriate tenants ; two splendid stags, very dark of coat, cantered at their stately leisure away from the line of our advance, and chirping flights of small birds—Moss Cheepers ?—like leaves on a gust, passed just overhead with a winnowing of little wings.

Hot as we made ourselves in the sheltered corrie, the gale and the cold were waiting for us as we reached the " col " leading to the main mass of the hill. The clouds were low, but not heavy and sullen ; ever and anon they broke and showed the cold blue behind, and beneath them stood massed that wonderful group of the Arrochar Highlands, whose names are in the hill-lover's ears like Milton's music of the Dorian mood,

> " Nor wanting power to mitigate and 'suage
> With solemn touches troubled thoughts, and chase
> Anguish, and doubt, and fear and sorrow and pain. "

—Ben Vane, Ben Ime, Narnain, a Chrois, Ben an Lochain, the Cobbler, and all that high society.

In that wild light their rugged shapes and the deep, steep-sided clefts between them were magnified and touched with tempestuous splendour. From the hidden sun slanted down long pencils of light that looked strange in their steadiness amidst the movement of the clouds and their shadows—in that furious gusty wind one would without immediate astonishment have seen them flicker. Glen Kinglass was flooded with a diffused, vague blur of gold that concealed all detail in a dim glory. But as though the spirits of the hills were jealous of these splendours, the fanged and battering wind made it impossible to stand and admire, and the fierce sting of hail on our faces was another goad. The fine, broken ridge was powdered with dry snow that here and there lay in the first diminutive drifts of the season ; this was no slush, but real wind-driven, frost-armoured snow. Winter had already occupied the summit as though to hold it against all counter-attacks from retiring autumn.

When we reached the first and lower cairn, the higher was hidden, but in accordance with the wild whim of the whistling, singing, cheering, hooting gale, the hail-cloud suddenly whirled away and a shaft of sunlight—how brilliant and how cold!—lit up the white ridge and the cairn proudly surmounting it.

From that untenable eminence we looked round for two minutes, gathering impressions of sights and sounds—hurrying cloud, steadfast sunrays, vapoury golden haze; tossed, defiant hill-shapes dimming already in the on-coming dusk; white-boulder strewn slopes around; the impressive plunge of the hillside down to Loch Sloy; Ben Lomond's proud ridge, from here thoroughly impressive; the darkening valley holding Loch Lomond, and above all the riot, the aggressive bitter cold, the sting and splendid invigoration of the north-west wind, triumphing as with sword and trumpet. Ten minutes more, and we were hurrying down through the sheltered corrie towards the few lights twinkling at the lochside, leaving the whitened crags to the gale and the night of stars.

It has been said by some authorities that after such an outing the best kind of bath is one tepid to start with, and gradually warmed up. They may be right; good enough for me has always been one as hot as I could bear it—not for long wallowing, but for a quick plunge, wash and splash about. The meal that follows should—for me—be ham-and-eggs and plenty of very sweet tea. Ah, those meals after a climb! No wonder that scoffers who have heard us lyrical about them have been known to say that we climb hills in uncomfortable weather chiefly for the sake of the joys of getting back and treating ourselves as heroes deserving every luxury.

An alternative to returning to Ardlui is to descend that steep slope down to Loch Sloy, and thence work down to Arrochar. It can be as wet a walk as you will find anywhere. I once did it on one of those days when grey clouds seem squeezing themselves out against the tops, and when the hills seem to have reached saturation point ; with me there was a touring youth whose plan had been to reach Arrochar by road, but who decided to accompany me on the more interesting way. He was not used to hills, and was wearing shoes, and I thought it very game of him. He was thrilled to see some ptarmigan and to catch a glimpse of deer through the whirling rain, and to have the experience of that kind of weather, which, from a very common point of view, could hardly have been worse.

By the time we reached Arrochar we were certainly thoroughly wet, but we were as happy as damp, and I think he enjoyed himself.

CHAPTER TWENTY-THREE

PERTHSHIRE'S BEN VORLICH

THIS grand hill is as well worth exploring as its namesake in Argyll; when I say " exploring " I mean to suggest that exploration includes the neighbourhood of each of the mountains, not just a walk up and down. One point in favour of the Perthshire Ben Vorlich is the interest of its approaches from several directions.

The simplest ascent is from Loch Earnside. Leaving the road about Ardvorlich, you go up the glen, escaping from it on to the open, firmer going of the long wide ridge that so obviously brings you to the summit, which reaches to 3,224 feet. It is a nicely-shaped top, actually something of a peak, and though not even a scramble is required to attain it, there is some grand rocky stuff all around. What an indescribably magnificent spot that can be in still, sunny weather ! Once in May two of us lunched, smoked and basked there amidst jumbled rocks and glittering snowdrifts, and found that an hour had passed and we were neither chilled nor weary of the view. Seldom have I been more sunburned—and the glow of the great fragrant banks of whin, in a glorious conflagration of blossom, through which we tramped later in Glen Keltie, seemed to carry on the roasting process.

If you have no intention of retracing your steps, and are prepared for a little more climbing and a ten-mile walk, you may turn north-westwards, and, having descended the long steepish slope of Vorlich, make for

Stuc a Chroin (3,189 feet)—a particularly fascinating
hill. I say " north-westwards " and not due west, to
save you a steep scramble down and up again. On the
east, Stuc a Chroin presents a long fringe of broken
cliffs, through which some quite easy gullies lead on
to the summit ridge. Those cliffs are quite spectacular,
and, half seen through cloud, can suggest a far greater
height than is actually theirs. The scenery of the
mountain is grand, and the trudge down to Arivurichardich—another gorgeous mouthful of a name !—
though long, is easy. From that farm a track,
practicable for a car I think, runs right down the
Keltie Water, with its Bracklinn Falls, into
Callander.

Should you choose to start from Callander—the
route I myself prefer—and the weather happens to be
thick when you are aloft, be a little careful which of
those gullies in the Stuc a Chroin battlement you choose
for your short-cutting descent towards Vorlich. They
all look much alike when you peer down them into
thick mist, but in some cases the lower part is much
steeper than in others. I remember once being with a
party, one of whom was fairly familiar with the hill,
while the others were complete strangers to its detail.
He, clambering down into what suggested a cloud-
filled abyss, sang out, " This is the one ! Come on, you
chaps," and disappeared, to hear from the mirk above,
a voice which firmly stated, " I wouldn't go down there
for five pounds ! "

The rest, sharing the hesitancy of this scorner of
money, took with him the long way round, following
the line of rocks till they flattened out, and, turning
their northern end, found the short cutter awaiting

them at the foot of the slope which led them all to Vorlich's cairn.

The gully-chooser had chosen right, and was consequently pleased with himself, only to be humbled on another occasion—this one marked by both cloud and a covering of snow. Again he paused at the top of a gully, assuring his single companion that this was an easy route down ; the companion, with some knowledge of mountains in general, failed to see how, under such conditions, the guide could be certain, and carried his point when he urged that they should move on till they reached a place where the crags were lower—and there, by-and-bye, they descended a gully which was the one the leader thought he had recognised a good deal higher up. I am not suggesting that they would have run any real risk had they tackled the first, but, since they chose to descend by glissading, they might have found a faster and bumpier slide than they looked forward to.

South-west of Stuc a Chroin is another top, Ben Each (Horse Hill ?) and it, too, has a character of its own, and its ascent brings the climber amongst really rugged surroundings. Further, I have an idea that this particular top—2,660 feet—is not frequently visited.

It was a cloudy day in May when a friend and I made the round trip I recommend. Leaving Callander, we walked up the road till we were near Arivurichardich, then turned left—there is a little bridge below the farm, over the Keltie Water—and got our steepest ascent over by getting up on to Sgiath an Dobrain. Here, as along the east flank of Stuc a Chroin, a line of quite impressive crags drops from the easy grass-and-boulder ridge by which you mount.

That neighbourhood has its own souvenir for me, for there we caught a Golden Plover chick—a perfectly beautiful little bird, gold-laced brown. It was not specially alarmed, and ran off none the worse after being held up and admired and photographed. (The photograph was of course no good ; but the bird lives in my memory, always a chick, with grey clouds and white-patched hills for its setting).

All around the summit of Ben Each—as the one-inch map shows very plainly—is a mazy jumble of cliffs and crags and boulders, all of which you can evade if you want to. It is rather a fascinating place, and would, I am sure, repay thorough exploration. In the circumstances in which we passed through it on that day it impressed me as having that uncompromisingly lonely atmosphere possessed inexplicably by some crannies amongst the mountains. A rushy lochan lies at the bottom of one of its hollows, and by it that day a fine stag was lying dead.

The snow, what was left of it, was patchy and softish, but we had a damp but amusing " sitting glissade" into the drop beyond, whence started the climb up to Stuc a Chroin, and presently everything around was snow and mist. My friend was the compass expert on this occasion—and it was just the very occasion to prove the usefulness of his lore, for it would have been quite natural to move off in an utterly wrong direction. There was not even a definite wind to keep us in our desired direction ; he wasn't far out, but a little, and instead of coming down the long slope from Stuc a Chroin we took the eastern flank of Ben Vorlich.

As we approached a burn in the cloudy gloaming, my thoughts were of the easy tramp down that Keltie

K

Water path with tub and grub at the end of it ; mentally I relaxed. When we reached the crossing-place, however, I saw nothing familiar there ; the tiny deserted building at the water's edge was certainly not Arivurichardich. I said so to my companion, and he told me what he thought I was aware of—that this stream wasn't the Keltie, but a tributary of the river which runs down Glenartney, and that to reach the road I had in mind we must " get over that "—and he pointed to slopes whose top was lost in cloud and darkness. It was nothing formidable after all ; a track gave its kindly guidance over the shoulder of the rise named Meal na h Iolaire, but that unexpected few hundred feet of climbing and those extra three miles put me altogether out of my reckoning, and I had not regained that contented feeling till we really did see Arivurichardich and the path below it. Then, I may say, we made a great march of it into Callander—with ham-and-eggs on the tow-rope.

And it is worth mentioning that as we strode down that path we met a couple of hikers upward bound, aiming to spend the night at the tiny shack I have mentioned, and be on their scrambling-ground when day broke.

Thinking of such as these, and those who pass their nights in such make-shift shelters as the Narnain Boulder, I salute the real hiker. He is often a tougher adventurer than anybody may suppose who sees him setting out from town with his crammed rucksack on his back.

That shack, by the way, stands in my retrospect with the name I gave to it when, close by, I realised that my mind had to tune up my body for an unex-

pected effort. " I'll call this place ' Psychological
Readjustment,' " I said, trying to be cheerful, to my
friend. I was thinking of a fact which has often struck
me, and, I daresay, everybody else who has occasion
to set his muscles and his staying-power a definite
task—it is that the mind seems to wind up the physical
powers for that definite task ; if, unexpectedly, the
mind directs the will to coerce the body into something
extra, that servant sometimes lags and indicates that
it would like to strike, as will, I understand, an elephant
if expected to work beyond its usual time.

I think this was recognised in the tougher training
of the war, when troops coming into camp after a
long day and expecting at once to relax and fall out,
were told that they had an extra mile or so to do.
Doubtless all-round training would in time make a
man almost unconscious of this " clock-watching "
habit of his body. Anyhow, most of us, have, I think,
realised it, and it is a curious and interesting phenomenon.

CHAPTER TWENTY-FOUR

BEN MORE

BEN MORE ; the Big Ben ; there are a number of
heights so-named about Scotland, but the one
near Crianlarich, in Perthshire, with its 3,843 feet, is
the highest. Some superior people say its height is
its only recommendation, and that it is just a great
lump. However, Ben More is a favourite of mine,
and further I can testify that particular conditions
can make its ascent worth anybody's while.

This point in its favour the most critical must
admit ; once you set foot on the mountain, which
really means the moment you leave the highroad if
you are aiming at climbing by the north face, every
step is upward. Ben More has no false crests, but
offers a straight forward, unremitting and, towards the
top, fairly steep slope. You see the montain well from
Crianlarich, a picture marred somewhat by the straight
line of the intervening railway-bridge.

About two-and-a-half miles east along the road
is Ben More farm. Having passed through the road-
gate beside it, look up ; then all you have to do is to
follow your nose.

From Crianlarich you will notice a great scoop in
the western side of the mountain ; along the side of
that mount the remains of an old dyke. In mist that
will serve you as a guide if you want one. If you
avail yourself of it, you should, however, leave it
before it fades out and continue a quarter-left. Not
doing so, you will find yourself confronted by nothing

serious, but by a fairly abrupt belt of mixed rock, grass, and moss, and may, if the cloud is thick, imagine yourself getting into difficulties.

Merely getting to the top of Ben More and coming down again may not be enough for you. What you can do to extend your outing is to make it an afternoon exercise, and then, during the night, walk down Loch Lomondside to Alexandria. I recommend the night for this, as during the day that road is of course the well-worn bed of a stream of traffic of all sorts.

Surely everybody would enjoy walking down Glen Falloch in the evening, then on towards Luss in the genial half-dusk of a summer night.

The route has only one drawback—the midges that assail you if you think you will take forty winks on one of those lovely little expanses of shingle. They are upon you in clouds after three minutes, and tobacco-smoke is no deterrent. (It did not occur to me ever to make a little damp-wood fire, and defend myself in its smoke—a " smudge " as the Canadian backwoodsmen call it. Anyhow I have an idea that our Highland midges laugh at such defences). I once found a brief spell of tranquillity and a half-snooze on a luggage-barrow under the bridge at Tarbet Station ; the midges for some reason did not follow me there. Such a vehicle is not however an ideal resting-place, for if the occupant is restless and alters his centre of gravity, the two-wheeled couch disconcertingly see-saws with a jolt.

Certain trivial episodes in walks remain vivid and refreshing long after others have faded, and so I recall, as if it happened yesterday, my approach to Luss one ideal morning in June. Everything seemed as fresh

as though newly-created ; birds and animals had
something of the boldness we imagine may have been
theirs in the age of innocence ; grass, leaves, flowers, all
wore a special cool radiance, and when presently little
feathers of smoke began to rise blue from chimneys
here and there, it was possible to imagine that the
dwellers lived happier lives than is the lot of mortals
anywhere.

After Luss, frankly, you walk for walking's sake
and to get to your destination, for the view you want
to see, of the loch on your left, is screened by a high
wall. I think the real satisfaction of that part of the
walk is anticipatory ; the trudger is buoyed up by the
thought of the pleasure of presently sitting down and
being transported for the rest of his journey.

A grand approach to Ben More is from the south,
that is to say from the road west of the head of Loch
Doine. The walk from Strathyre is as pleasant a one
as you could wish, if you feel like that preface to the
seven or eight miles switchback I am proposing for you.
The first height you must attain is Stob Invercarnaig,
some 2,300 feet high, and then you are on a perfectly
delightful wide grassy ridge which gently rises to 3,497
feet in Stob Coire an Lochain, with very little dip before
the peakish top of Am Binnein, commonly called
Stobinian. Then you see the south front of Ben More
challenging you across a considerable dip of something,
I am afraid, like a thousand feet. But it is worth
while ; that slope of Ben More is fairly steep and
boulder-strewn, interesting ground, and brings you to
the Ben More cairn without any serious interruptions.

Descending a slope such as Ben More's front is,
to me and I think many another, what we least like

doing in the hills. For one reason, it means anti-climax ; for another, it is more tiring, to the feet at least, than going up. Under certain conditions it can be really annoying. I once came down, when the grass was wet and slippery in places, with a big man wearing the kilt and smooth-soled shoes. Ever and anon one of his feet shot from under him, and he sat down with an earth-shaking thump and a loud word, on the cold and soggy slope.

In this neighbourhood there are several perfect ridge-walks, as the map will indicate to you there must be.

Starting from the south, you can make the " traverse " over Ben Tulaichean (3,099 feet), Cruach Ardrain (3,428 feet), and Stob Coire Buidhe (2,806 feet) ; or take the left fork of the ridge structure at Cruach Ardrain and go down by Grey Height ; and there are similar opportunities to the immediate west.

Having done these high walks from the south, do them again from the north, and see what variety the change of direction purveys.

Some walkers will, I know, recommend parallel tramps down in the glens between the ridges. All right for those who like that sort of thing, but to some of us the sense of being shut in, not to mention the usual soppiness underfoot, makes such routes not worth comparison with the high ground where the wind and the wide prospects, and the firmer footing are—and few flies care to follow.

Ben More is, like all hills, a completely different proposition under really wintry conditions, which are often a feature of March or April. Let me confess that twice, once with a friend and once alone, this lump of a hill has defeated me.

Once it was in April, when the low-lying snow was already softening. The higher we went, the harder was the snow, and mightier grew the force of the wind. I suppose we kept too far to the right ; at any rate we found ourselves up against a steep rise with ice-covered rock just under the frozen moss. Patience would have negotiated this all right, of course, but with the gale dazzling and pelting us with furiously-driven blizzards of snow-dust, dry as blown sand and as sharp, that was no time or place for patience to have a chance. The gale seemed to come from every direction at once, on eddies snow blew up our noses and stung our eyes ; it whirled from above, and eddies from which there was no shelter, between our legs. The pick end of our axes made no impression on that rocky surface, which gave no hold for boot-nails. Moreover we had to think of a train to catch, and the daylight was passing. So we gave up and made our way down the eastern slopes, where the snow was drifted and soft. There, knee-deep, we halted presently for a sandwich and a breather, and tried to rid our woolly balaclavas of their fringes of clinging half-melted ice.

My solitary disgrace had very nearly the same place for its scene. It was on one glorious January day when Crianlarich and its neighbourhood wore the perfect Christmas Card aspect. The high-road to Ben More farm presented laborious going, so thick was the snow. I feared it might be deeper higher up, but ought to have known better, considering the east wind that, even on the level, was blowing strongly in my face.

Looking up, I could see snow driving like smoke across the front of the hill, and as I rose I realised that

W.K.H.

THE HEAD OF GLEN FALLOCH

the wind was sweeping the open ground clear, and dropping the driven snow round the shoulder and letting it accumulate in every depression.

Partly in the vain hope of escaping its full force, I kept too far right, and got at last to that steeper, rockier, slippery rise mentioned above. In spite of my exertions I was very cold, and decided to get out an extra woolly from my rucksack. To do so I removed my gloves, and almost at once my hands were so stiff with cold that the negotiation of straps, buckles, and buttons was beyond them. Then, to hamper me still further, the gale seemed to choose that moment to indulge in a special outbreak, and everything loose, including the rucksack which I was struggling to replace over my shoulders, thrashed about quite beyond control. Further, my eyes were streaming with tears, which made it impossible to see where next to plant a foot.

Thinking it all made too much of a good thing, once again I decided to let the mountain win, and turned. Had I chosen a line just a little further east, this disgrace would not have had to be confessed. And of course I might have descended a short distance and made a cast across, into the teeth of the wind, and then changed direction and made for the top. All very true, and those were the things I told myself when, a few hundred feet down, I found a boulder's lee and was able to think, unbattered by that flaying wind; but, while you are the plaything of such a wind, calm reflection isn't easy. The next time conditions are like that, and I don't want to be defeated, I shall set out wearing as much clothing as can be required high up.

If anybody who reads this confession thinks that

a man must be soft to retire from dear old Ben More,
I think he reveals the fact that he cannot have tackled
the hill when it was in a thoroughly rampageous mood.
Since that day of defeat Ben More made wonderful
amends.   It was on the one fine day in a spell of most
melancholy weather.   Despite low-clinging mist, I set
out for a leisurely plod upwards, and at about 3,000
feet emerged suddenly into glorious sunshine under a
clear sky, the brilliance of which was dazzlingly reflected from a level plain of fleecy cloud stretching for
miles in all directions, pierced near and far by peaks
clear in every detail.   Visibility was such that from the
top I could see from Ben Nevis to the Ochils, and
conditions so genial that a Red Admiral butterfly was
flitting at his own sweet will about the cairn.

CHAPTER TWENTY-FIVE

BEN DORAN

BEN DORAN—or Dorain—(3524 feet) is a mountain that surely has arrested many an eye normally blind to mountain-shapes, since, from the highroad or the railway running north from Tyndrum, it rises in a regular and dominant pyramid challenging the attention of the most unobservant. Its shape is not at all that of a pyramid, as you find when you reach the summit or observe it from other angles, but that is its best-known and most characteristic profile.

It has the distinction of having been celebrated in song by the Gaelic bard Duncan Ban Macintyre, whose words, I understand, indicate that in his day parts of it were wooded.

Though I have enjoyed some excellent days which included Ben Doran, it is not amongst my favourite hills. Yet I like the abruptness of the slope by which it rises above the U-bend on the railway, and the approach to the top amongst its rock-ridges, and of course its position makes it a superb viewpoint in clear weather. On a day of drifting broken cloud, too, I have seen some startling effects when a sudden rent in the grey masses revealed road, railway, and river, a miniature landscape, very nearly straight below—or so it seemed. As for that slope, I have heard it referred to as the steepest grass slope in Scotland ; steep it certainly is, but the turf, towards the top, is only skin-deep, and so to me the descent is irritating, neither one thing nor the other. Better fun than a return by that ridge is the descent of one of the gullies on the long western face of the mountain. By using one of them you escape the unpleasant "bony" footing of the southerly front, and can have a little very easy scrambling.

Ben Doran is a grand hill; to realise how grand, try to visualize that neighbourhood without his presence. Under snow it is particularly magnificent to look at—and that when it lies deep and hard those who like step-cutting and a really long glissade would find all they could desire upon its proudly-rising flanks.

Ben Achallader (on the map Achadh-fhaladair), 3,399 feet, to the north, is characterised chiefly by the great sweep of the braes up from the railway line—steep slopes which offer a good test for your condition. It is worthy of attention, and when you have climbed it you might as well include Ben an Dothaidh (Dough); they are not however amongst the hills which have, for me, any particular appeal.

Perhaps this is only because I have never been on them except in that sort of weather which is neither one thing nor the other; just dull and damp, with no distant view and no great wind or snow or marching columns of rain to give the touch of drama which mountains owe to wild weather.

Livelier conditions might have left me with a totally different impression, and every time I travel by the Highland line and look up at those towering slopes I am glad I have been in a position to look down.

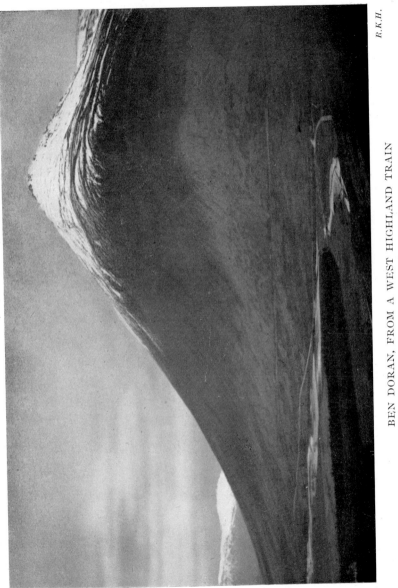

R.K.H.

BEN DORAN, FROM A WEST HIGHLAND TRAIN

CHAPTER TWENTY-SIX

SCHIEHALLION AND THE GLEN LYON HILLS

A WONDERFUL walk, if you can face thirty miles, is that from Fortingall right through Glen Lyon, and then past Loch Lyon and along the Allt Chonoglais —which is the stream that runs under the bridge in the railway loop a few miles north of Tyndrum—till you reach the highroad. A great day's march ; but why not take it in sections at your leisure ? Both sides of that marvellous glen are hills demanding attention, if you must have hills.

I have gossiped about Ben Lawers and its neighbours elsewhere in these pages, so will say nothing about them under this heading. To include Schiehallion (3547 feet) may seem a little far-fetched. It is, however, associated in my mind with Glen Lyon, if only because I made the mountain's acquaintance while en route for the Glen.

My first ascent of Schiehallion was unsatisfactory for several reasons, one being that I did not give myself time, and after a rough-rider's lift on the back of a motor-cycle, took a rather absurd and wearisome line for the hill, plugging up the northern flank with a rucksack heavier than I care to carry. The day was neither one thing nor the other, and I tramped down the long and stony eastern ridge somehow disillusioned with a hill I had so often admired from distant points of view, whence it presented itself as a peak, not as the long hog-back it actually is.

Later I changed my opinion. Schiehallion is

supposed to owe its name to some sort of association with the Schie—the Good Folk, the Fairies. It is also believed to attract lightning, and I have been told that shepherds like to get their charges off its top when thunder is about. It certainly has the distinction of having, thanks to its isolated bulk, served early scientists as a standard by which they arrived at an estimate of the weight of the earth—an estimate which more recent investigators have declared to be not far wrong.

As to its fairies I cannot say anything, having no experience, but its summit can be, I know, a good spot for varied weather. During the windy ten minutes a friend and I spent lunching there one spring day, we experienced sunshine, a rain-shower, a snow-squall, thunder, and lightning.

After my first visit I spent the night at Coshieville Inn, and heard a good local ghost story from a man who said it happened to himself, and was as true as that he was sitting there, which he certainly was.

I went to church at Dull the following morning, and learned a good deal; amongst other things that the name is not descriptive—nobody could surely suppose it after a visit to the vicinity—but that of course it was based on a Gaelic word referring to the litter in which the dying saint Conan was carried. At Dull the litter broke down, and so that was the spot at which, according to the wishes of Conan, a religious establishment was set up; I was also informed that there is still an eccelesiastical connection between Dull and St. Andrews itself, and that Dull claims, in a sense, seniority over that parish as a seat of Christian learning. I am not writing history, but repeating what was told me by a member of the congregation who saw me part of my way back to Coshieville.

That afternoon I decided on an easy daunder towards Creag Mhor, a plain grassy height rising to just over 3,000 feet, not caring whether I reached the highest point or not. I emphasise my mood and lack of intention to prove that I wasn't pressing myself.

Well, then, my heart wasn't pumping or my ears drumming, so the little incident which befell is not to be explained as due to blood pressure or cardiac palpitation. The afternoon was warm and sunny, with just a pleasant little breeze—an afternoon less "spooky" or encouraging to spooky fancies no summer ever produced. What befell was odder in its effect on me than can be justified by a description of the incident :
— I can best indicate of what I was conscious by saying that as I plodded happily and lazily up the open brae it was as if something or somebody had suddenly stamped hard twice on the short dry turf at my back ; and its effect was to make me clammy under my shirt.

No sheep was anywhere near, and it would have needed a monster sheep to stamp like that. Perhaps a boulder in an underground cavity had, for some reason, fallen over ; perhaps a miniature earth-tremor had occurred. I thought of such explanations, and went on, but the atmosphere of the afternoon had lost something of its cheerfulness.

I always make the most of that trivial occurrence, which has, of course, some natural explanation—but if it had *seemed* natural, why on earth was my body's reaction to turn cold ?—because it is the only slightly queer thing, apart from the physical, that has ever happened to me alone on a hill; and because it so often produces a far better story in the same line, and has served to introduce the whole subject of the spookiness of the Glen Lyon neighbourhood. A Highlander has assured me it was most certainly a psychic experience; the whole area, Killin especially, being, according to him, a great haunt of earth-bound spirits, kept there as a consequence of their connection with many deeds of blood; was not a friend of his struck by an invisible hand somewhere near Fearnan?

I have been assured that the immediate vicinity of the church at Killin is, by the psychic, notably frequented by more than others perceive, but though I have loafed around there at dusk I could not raise a perceptive shiver. If there are indeed haunted buildings, surely the ruins of Finlarig Castle, just at the head of Loch Tay, ought to be amongst them. Even in broad warm daylight it impressed me as uncanny, and the legends about it would well justify its frequentation by a gory ghost or two. Though apparitions of that sort may deny themselves to you, there you may feel compensated by an amusing piece of sculpture. The story is that troublesome wives used to be taken by their husbands to contemplate it as a warning; it represents a man spanking his spouse.

One yarn leads to another, particularly a spooky yarn, even amongst the professedly most sceptical. I had begun to tell the story of my " scare " on Creag Mhor to a most level-headed, athletic type, when he interrupted me by a Glen Lyon yarn of his own. He had set out to fish one of the burns that the hills send down as contributions to the River Lyon, but his angler's morning brightness was dulled by an indefinable

W.K.H.

LOOKING UP GLEN LYON

unease of mind ; then things began to go wrong, little things, but, in the aggregate, more than merely annoying, and presently he came to a kind of hollow with white stones in it where he felt so strongly that he was not wanted that he straightway turned and went down, giving up his fishing for the day.

I refer to these yarns because some people like to believe there is something other than a commonplace "natural" explanation for them, and certainly brooding on them when you are alone, letting some old instincts have their say from the ancient dark, can add an interest to a walk amongst the hills. I'm afraid I can't take them with any seriousness myself. All the phantoms that ever stood in my path in the gloom of the night have disappointingly transformed themselves, when approached, into white boulders, or little waterfalls, or wavering columns of vapour. Even the seven little men in peaked caps who kept pace for me for quite a distance in the mist on the Campsies—so definitely marching dwarfs that I half expected them to burst out singing " Off to work we go ! "—became at length tin-hooded posts round a boggy hole, much nearer to me than the dwarfs had seemed.

It is high time I lead you properly into Glen Lyon, but I must pause for a word about Fortingall. Everybody knows that it—or the Roman camp near—is the reputed birthplace of Pontius Pilate ; everybody knows of its ancient yew-tree ; but I have never met anyone who has shared my inquisitiveness about a little rough stone obelisk, a miniature monolith, that stands in the field opposite the hotel.

To me that stone, and the inscription on it, are wonderfully evocative. " Carn na Marbh "—Cairn of

L

the Dead — reads the lettering ; " Here lie victims of the Great Plague of the 14th Century. Taken here on a sledge drawn by a white horse and led by an old woman."

I wonder why somebody thought it worth while to mention the colour of the horse, and am delighted that somebody did, and if ghosts do wander around, I hope that old woman's can thrill with pride to find herself with a monument, even an anonymous one.

Well, there is grand wandering-ground all the way along both sides of this lovely glen. It was while coming down from Cairn Mairg that a friend and I saw deer in numbers greater than I thought ever collected in one area. They had gathered in a corrie, hundreds of them ; the " troop " of forty we counted was just a unit of the multitude. I most vividly remember the one, slower than its companions, that limped as it passed across our front.

Glen Lyon has its unexpected features, one of which is the great pool at the Bridge of Balgie, where comes down the road from Loch Tayside ; and its suddenly-opening level green straths are others. Having been driven, on one occasion, pretty nearly as far as Loch Lyon, I made a divergence and took in Beinn Mhanach, a not particularly interesting hill of 3,125 feet ; in those days I was " collecting Munros," and was vexed with myself, later on, for not having noticed that with very little trouble I could have bagged another, Ben a Chuirn. This is mentioned for the benefit of any reader who is under the spell of that youthful enthusiasm.

The map indicates the site of an ancient chapel on the west bank of the stream that runs below the flank of Ben Doran ; I looked for but failed to find any trace of it. That stretch of a pretty rough path is associated in my memory with the sound of a hollow knocking which reached my ears from the crags near the summit of Doran. It suggested the banging together of a couple of boulders, and puzzled me. Could there be somebody hurt up there, trying to attract attention ? Ought I to clamber up and find out ? I was tired by now, and had a train to catch at Tyndrum, and reflected that nobody but a giant could produce, in that way, a noise to reach me so distinctly three thousand feet below. I walked on, puzzling until I turned the corner and, emerging from the glen, had a view across to the new road beyond the railway. There a roller was at work, and my knocking rocks from Ben Doran were echoes from the racket it was making.

Ben Heasgarnich (accent on the first syllable), 3,550 feet, might be included amongst the Glen Lyon hills. I have done it only from the Glen Lochay side, and found it an interesting hill with great possibilities for bewilderment in cloud. On its summit start several burns, no two running in the same direction, and it would be only too easy to accept a wrong one as guide. From that top you get a new idea of the true shape of Doran, and perhaps learn a new respect for that mountain.

CHAPTER TWENTY-SEVEN

BUCHAILLE ETIVE MOHR

THIS magnificent mountain mass presents its noblest and most formidable aspect to the north and east, where it culminates in the peak of Stob Dearg (3,345 feet), seen from the neighbourhood of Kingshouse Hotel as a rough pyramid. Its name is so closely associated with certain famous rock-climbs—the Crow-berry Ridge for example—that the humble scrambler may be completely scared off, and assume that it is a mountain to which he need not aspire.

Such diffidence is of course quite uncalled-for. Even on that scarred eastern face, so beautiful in the full light of the morning sun, so awesome in the gloom of sombre weather, there are " easy " climbs. My first visit to Buchaille was made by a route known to mountaineers as " The Curved Ridge," and how lightly we took it—under a couple of expert leaders—may be gathered from the fact that there was general agreement that on such a day—warm and tranquil, with the rocks dry—the rope was perhaps superfluous.

By the cairn we had our lunch, basking in the splendour of the day, perched on one mountain wave-tip amongst a tossed ocean of them. I remember that lunch particularly, because somebody had thought it worth while to include several tins of peaches with the plainer grub, and as there were lingering clean little drifts in an adjacent cranny, we improved each half-peach with a pinch of snow.

We descended into Glen Etive by what is called

W.K.H.

THE BIDEAN NAM BIAN GROUP, FROM BUCHAILLE

Coire Cloiche Finne. The top of this is about 400 yards west of the Buchaille cairn, and, to avoid difficulties, you are advised to keep to the right-hand side. It is stony enough whatever route you pick—a most irregular staircase of carelessly flung boulders. We did it, for some reason or no reason, at a rush, and, reaching the Etive just where a glorious pool invited, tore off our scanty sweat-soaked garments and revelled in the sparkling water, emerging fresh as paint for the walk back to Kingshouse.

I dislike descending hills, though I recognise that anyone who likes climbing them must reconcile himself to the reverse activity, and that stony Coire seems to me much more agreeable to go up than to come down. An alternative easy scramble is from the north side, from Altnafeadh on the Glencoe Road. Also there seems no reason why the vigorous walker should not cover the whole group from south-west to north-east, from a point about five miles up Glen Etive.

CHAPTER TWENTY-EIGHT

BEN Y GLOE

I THINK a good many would agree with me that for easy, delightful hill-climbing there is perhaps no area to surpass that east of Glen Tilt, which contains the group of tops with the general name of Ben Y Gloe. There you attain a satisfactory height—over 3,000 feet —without any rough work at all.

Blair Atholl is the best " base." When I had my first walk in that neighbourhood, my friend and I took the most southerly top, Carn Liath (3,193 feet) first, reaching it by following a path which passes the Falls of Fender, and leads to the top of little Loch Moraig, whence a much less definite track indicates the further route. Paths, however, you will not want, once you are clear of the farms and trees. These hills are not bad for bracken, which on others—the lower slopes of Cruachan, for instance—can in autumn slow up your progress considerably, either uphill or down.

From that top there is a considerable descent, still, however, gentle going, before you start uphill again for Chruinn Chalgain, a fine upstanding hill of 3,505 feet. Carn nan Gabhar is the top to the east, and worth including for every reason—it is also a " Munro," with a handsome margin, its height being 3,671 feet. The going is so grassy, everywhere on this group, and most of the gradients so gradual, that you will hardly believe you have attained so high.

The views from these hills are really magnificent, particularly to the north. They are entertaining, too, with their wild life—deer, ptarmigan, hawks included.

From Carn na Gabhar we took a line nearly due north, which brought us down into Glen Tilt, so that we had a most agreeable walk of eight miles or so, all gently downhill, by a track that presently becomes one of the nicest grass roads I know. I recommend Glen Tilt with all my heart, whether you bother with the mountains around it or not. The enterprising pedestrian who likes a really long walk can go right up Glen Tilt, over the level watershed at about 1,500 feet, and then down into Deeside and Braemar. I think that most alluring expedition could be done on pony-back ; what a ride !

The aspect of the valley, as you approach it down the lower part of Glen Tilt, is one you will not easily forget if you have an eye for scenery. We were lucky that day, for the evening was calm and sunny, and a glow transfused the air, lending the opening vista all the beauty of light and shade.

Our next expedition was aimed at Ben Dearg (3,304 feet), and as our route we chose the path that runs along the Bruar Water, which unites with the Garry about three miles west of Blair Atholl. That is another walk not to be missed. The gorge of the Bruar is slightly too well supplied with nicely-made paths and view-points for those who don't like scenery prepared for the tourist, but nothing could spoil it—so long as the river runs.

The rocky gorge is fine ; so are the trees, and Burns enthusiasts will be pleased to remember that their presence is due to the Bard who, visiting it when it was treeless, plead poetically—and effectively—with the Duke of Atholl to do some planting.

That gorge is the only place in Scotland, incidentally, where I have heard the jay, and had a glimpse of the gorgeous bird, and I have seen it there on two occasions, calling attention to itself more by its harsh outcries than by its brilliant plumage.

We followed the road for about six miles, till just short of Bruar Lodge, then cut off and made for the hill by the wide grassy ridge climbing to the summit from the south. Our luck with the weather was not so good on this day ; the sky was overcast, and on the high ground the wind extremely bitter for July. That top is a bouldery one, and if you have any interest at all in geology and know the Cairngorms, you will hail as an old friend the granite that appears there, quite a different rock from that of the rest of the mountain ; a geological map will confirm the correctness of your impression. It was too chilly for us to stand long either geologising or admiring the view, which was bleak, in any case, under that dull sky. Heading south, we followed the ridge right down, and presently struck a path which brought us most comfortably down the course of the Allt an t Seapail, to join the road through wooded Glen Banvie, through the grounds of Blair Castle—we hoped we were not exactly intruding—and so back to Blair Atholl.

Any number of expeditions will suggest themselves to anybody who studies that part of the map of Scotland ; it is country that pleads for the foot of the wanderer.

CHAPTER TWENTY-NINE

AMONGST THE CAIRNGORMS

THE Cairngorms ; there is magic in the name—- magic whose power strengthens with knowledge of the area it represents. How anybody, seeing them say from Aviemore station, amethyst in the evening light, can resist their allurement, I cannot understand. And the more you know of them, the more you want to know, and the field for exploration which they offer is surely inexhaustible.

Visiting them first, anyone familiar with the western Scottish hills will find them in almost every way utterly different. Geology, amongst other agencies, has taken care of that ; the whole massif called the Cairngorms is the rubbed down base of granite moun- tains rising, it is surmised, to a height many times that of Macdhui, their highest point, 4,296 feet. Their glens and passes and lochans are, presumably, the result of denudation since the ice scraped down the original giants. Even their colour is very different from that of, say, the Nevis group, while the summits of most of them tend to the form of plateaux.

For the walker they present their own problems, the chief of which is the distance of the big hills from villages or even dwellings or roads. To have " a day on the Cairngorms " you must be prepared to cover a good many miles before you are on or amongst the hills at all. The wise are of course those who make their base a tent, or one of the famous bothies, or the Shelter Stone at the head of Loch Avon. It is possible, however, with the aid of a car, to do a good deal between sunrise and sunset on a summer day.

My first dash for Macdhui—a dash it was—would have been impossible for me but for transport from Aviemore as far as Coylum Bridge—a spot which might be called the Charing Cross of the Cairngorms. Anybody waiting there long enough would see most of his hill-frequenting acquaintances sooner or later.

The road from Coylum Bridge to Loch Morlich makes for its own sake a walk not on any account to be missed. You must choose sunshine for it, for without sunshine the magnificent old Scots pines which are the glory of this whole countryside do not display the glowing richness of their rough ruddy bark, with its contrast to that of the deep green foliage, nor do you see the wonderful pale colour of the Loch Morlich sands. Scots pines, juniper, heather, and blaeberry ; these give the landscape its special character.

Beyond the loch I found the start of the Cairngorm path rather hard to find, but trusting my map I cut across some open ground and found it, a most delightful track mounting through trees by the Allt More. Outside the woods it climbs more steeply, and comes to an end at a Bench Mark at 2,117 feet. Beyond that nobody would expect a path ; a shoulder runs up between two burns, about a couple of miles up and on you reach the summit of Cairngorm, 4,064 feet. From there I made for Macdhui, some four miles off, with roughish going. The day was moderately good, and no time was wasted in checking the route; that was obvious. I am not proud of that outing ; it was so hurried that it left me with only a very mixed impression of those high places.

Cloud was low enough to be just clearing most of the tops, but its skirts were trailing across the summit of Macdhui, veiling the cairn as I approached. Under such conditions any stony mountain can look bleak, and even a trifle desolate and eerie : I was well up in the lore of the Ferla Mhor—the Great Grey Man—who is supposed to haunt the mountain, but, imagine as I might, I could discern nothing more phantom-like than those drifting wreaths.

As to the Grey Man, some of the stories are told with impressive circumstantiality. One of the best describes how two men were on Macdhui one moonlight night, separated by some distance from one another. When they joined, one said to his friend, " That was surely a terrific big chap who came up and passed near you—he looked to me taller than the cairn." "What chap ? " was the answer. " I saw nobody except you, and you were nowhere near the cairn."

That famous climber, the late Professor Collie, is generally associated with the Grey Man. He is supposed to have seen him, to have heard his tread, and seen his footsteps in the snow. So when a party of us found the Professor amongst our fellow-guests at Sligachan Hotel, I was all ears when one member ventured to ask him what his eerie experience had really been. The annoying thing about that incident is that though he told us we can't say we exactly know, because the evidence of the hearers differs in one essen-tial. One of his listeners maintains that Collie said he he heard footsteps ; I am—almost—prepared to swear that he said no such thing, but merely admitted that one day, alone on the snow-sprinkled summit, he was seized with a panic for which there was no apparent reason, and no subsequent explanation, but which was real enough to set him off at a run, which didn't drop to a walk till he had covered a long, long distance.

Professor Collie's experience of mountains all over the world helps to make the Macdhui episode interesting, from various points of view. Such moments of panic, varying in degree, are not as rare as might be supposed by those not conversant with the reminiscences of roamers in solitary places. Wordsworth may have experienced something of the kind, to inspire him to write:—

> " I heard among the solitary hills
> Low breathings coming after me, and sounds
> Of undistinguishable motion, steps
> Almost as silent as the earth we trod. "

Yet this suggests something too definite—the more common fear is produced by nothing that could be described as breathings, motion, steps.

Let us say it is due to a sudden realization of loneliness, and not worry about the persistence of those who will point out that something of the kind has been experienced by two people together.

My second ascent of Cairngorm was, I regret to say, also in a hurry, but it was in livelier weather, and left me with a glorious memory of blustery sunshine, rainbows, rainclouds, shining wet rock, glowing mosses, to represent the hill, and of Loch Morlich, with its background of mountains, so marvellous that home-ward bound I walked backwards for the first part of the lochside road, despite the risk of tripping over pine-tree roots. The hills were a many-coloured blur of sunshine and dark thunder-cloud, and the foreground, sparkling and brilliant after intermittent showers, made a picture which would have pleased even the idealist as representing Scotland at its most beautiful.

I had that day tried a short cut from Loch Morlich, instead of finding the path. Believe me, it is not worth it for anybody in a hurry. I found myself thrusting my way amongst trees upright and fallen, through great jungles of heather and blaeberry, and across miniature canyons, where, it would have been easy to believe, nobody had ever been before. And I remember being particularly struck by the stoutness of the cobwebs outstretched here and there, as though the place was the habitat of a race of giant spiders.

Perhaps my best Cairngorm day was a blazing August one with a local man who seemed to have made the mountain remotenesses his second home. Here and there he had made caches of oatmeal, so that in an emergency he would never be many miles from something which would sustain life. He was the kind of chap who liked to bring in the New Year at the upper bothy in Glen Einich, whither he and his friends would tow their needs on a sleigh. That day we drove as far as the gate across the Glen Einich road, and went for the main cairn of Braeriach (4,248 feet) by the steep and rocky slopes south of Loch Coire an Lochain, a hot scramble on that broiling day. That lochan, and the crags around it, make a wild and impressive piece of scenery, but to reach them demands some real exertion ; notice on the map how close the contour-lines run, and if you start, do not be surprised. There are no difficulties, however.

What an astonishing plateau is that summit of Braeriach, miles of it at an elevation never far below the several tops that surmount the four-thousand foot level! It is all granite and tiny mosses, strewn in autumn with the white drifting down of the seeds of that tiniest of all trees, the dwarf mountain willow ; blue sky and blazing sunshine, and the feeling of real wide expanse and sparkling air and ability to go on for ever over that clean rock—such are my memories of Braeriach on a radiant day.

Yes, but a change of weather, a different season, transforms it to something as different as night from day. Those who tackle the Cairngorms, and perhaps in particular Braeriach, between late autumn and late spring must treat them with respect, as various fatalities have demonstrated. Up there conditions can be comparable with the Arctic regions, and this should be borne in mind even by the hardiest and most venturesome.

After pausing awhile to cool, and eat, and admire the wide-spread view—as well as that down into the great corries plunging down into the Larig, and called by some " The Porridge Corrie," we turned and trudged across that stony, airy wilderness for the Einich Cairn and the little shallow pools amongst the stones which are called the Wells of Dee. Thence—how easily it is written !—we did a further march of a couple of miles or so and reached the summit of Cairntoul (4,241 feet). The glorious day was wearing away and we had still a long way to go, and so we aimed for the depths of the Larig, cutting down by the shoulder east of Lochain Uaine. The name means " Little Green Loch " ; that day, I remember, it shone like an emerald in its high setting amongst the grim crags.

As, standing near the cairn, we decided on our route down into the Larig, I thought of the descent as

an easy matter, to occupy perhaps half an hour ; was
it not all down-hill ? Downhill, certainly ; very much
so ; but every step on that slope—not much else than a
great stone-shoot—has to be taken with a certain
carefulness, and my half-hour proved a fantastic under-
estimate ; in fact it seemed as though we should never
reach the bed of the pass and the path.

When we did, we found the Larig hot like a summer-
house, every stone baking under that noble sun, and the
heather's purple glowing. Purple ? Not far from the
Pools of Dee we found a great cushion of heather pure
white—luck enough for a hundred, if we had needed
more luck than such a day. I picked a spray or two of
that, but my best souvenir of that tramp is the tiny
feather dropped by a ptarmigan as she with her young
family got off the path, in no particular hurry, and no
such undignified outcries as are commonly given forth
by the domestic fowl in such circumstances.

I confess I was weary that evening, after the hours
of tramping and scrambling in the heat of a glowing
August day, but my younger companion attended a
local dance. I suppose he would want to settle his
supper.

My memories of another of the Cairngorms,
Sgor Gaoith (3,658 feet) overlooking Loch Einich on
the west, are of a very different kind. It is a grand
hill, with magnificent cliff-scenery where it drops
precipitately to the lochside. On a really gloomy day
the cliffs round the head of the loch can be justly
described as grim and forbidding. That day our little
party saw them first in sunshine as we walked up the
Glen, and then, picking an easy way on to the high
ground, followed up the ridge to the summit, but

before noon the aspect of the mountains changed. The
sun disappeared and a darkness gathered on the tops,
deepening as we descended till, looking back, we saw
that the massed cloud was pressing lower and lower.
We hurried, but hurrying was in vain. Rain began,
heavy rain, but a downpour that must have been
nothing to what was happening about the hidden
summits. That lowering cloud-mass was like a sponge,
and like a squeezed sponge it discharged its watery
contents into every burn. The river, after a few
minutes, became a terrific spectacle, and the scene all
around was a startling illustration of denudation in
violent action. Every little stream pouring across our
way was thick and deeply coloured, and in its headlong
descent carried with it stones that were worthy of the
name of boulders. Tons of solid material must have
been washed down within an hour, and the turgid,
hurtling river bore towards the valley a burden of loot
that was the substance of the mountains. No wonder
that in the course of ages the face of the earth alters,
with such agencies incessantly at work.

By the time we got back to Aviemore we had
walked ourselves nearly dry again, for the rain soon
ceased after that terrific onslaught.

I am deeply sorry to say I have never been amongst
the Cairngorms when they were under snow ; then
they must be like a country to themselves. The whole
area offers scope for so much exploration, for tramping
and climbing of so many varieties, that the ordinary
man, with limited leisure for such undertakings, might
devote a life-time to the Cairngorms alone, and not
exhaust their novelty.

CHAPTER THIRTY

LOCHNAGAR

LOCHNAGAR is a grand mountain in every respect, and well deserves its triumphant name and Byron's poem. As to that poem, incidentally, I never find it in my head without seeing not only Lochnagar's magnificent cliffs, but also some of the savagery of the rock shapes around Wastdalehead in Cumberland. The most patriotic Scot, placed suddenly in certain spots amongst the gullies plunging down from Scawfell, for instance, could never after maintain that the whole truth was contained in the sweeping statement that England's beauties were " tame and domestic."

I know that Lakeland area in various kinds of weather, smiling and scowling, glittering with snow and smothered in sombre drenching rain-clouds ; Lochnagar was the reverse of dark each time I climbed it. To me it is a mountain basking in the sunshine. I have always had weather-luck on this mountain, with the " bonus " of superb views in every direction. Also I must confess that I have done it only in luxurious fashion, transported by car to the starting point of a good clear path that leads up from Glen Muick. In such weather no mountain lore is needed, only sufficient staying-power to keep on walking. The only steepish portion of the path is near the top, where a certain ascent is known as The Ladder—but even here there is no question of using your hands as well as your feet. The zig-zags of the Ladder were, I believe, engineered on Queen Victoria's behalf.

I doubt if there is a mountain-top on the mainland of Scotland with a more majestic air. The twin summits, less than half a mile apart, and with less than twenty feet in height between them [Cac Carn Mor (3,768 feet), and Cac Carn Beag (3,786 feet)] stand out on a bold " promontory," with cliffs all round, and with an awe-inspiring corrie, each with its Lochan, on the left hand and on the right.

The rock-formations are such as to attract detailed exploration—here are great piled slabs, in some cases reminiscent of the " Cyclopean Wall " on Goatfell, and masses weathered into fantastic shapes that through mist must put on the likeness of monsters from a nightmare.

In the superb weather that indulged us—windless and warm as well as gorgeously sunny—it was possible to linger in comfort, lunching, wandering here and there, and identifying some of the innumerable hill-tops visible in every direction. We saw as far as the Ochils and the Pentlands. Always, from those far landmarks, dim under the blue sky, the eye would return to the noble plunge of the precipices into the near corries. The water of Lochnagar mirrors the sky from more than a thousand feet below your stance up there amongst the great boulders of the summit.

Most assuredly, when once you reach that grand mountain-top, and conditions are such as I have described, you will not want to hurry away ; I think one could well spend the whole of a summer day, from sunrise to sunset, absorbing the sunshine, inhaling that exhilarating golden air, and noting how the movement of shadows revealed new features in the immense landscape.

When at last you must conquer your reluctance and abandon the heights, you can return by the easy way which led you up or you can take the path which runs along the top of the corrie to the west, and then winds amongst the hills till it joins the track which runs down Glen Callater into Braemar. Glen Callater is well worth seeing for its own sake, but that route from Lochnagar means a trek of at least eleven miles, of which the first part, though on a path, must count as double its map-length for your legs.

Lochnagar is magnificent in snow, its constant frequenters tell me and I well believe them.

CHAPTER THIRTY-ONE

SGURR BAN

M Y experience of Sgurr Ban (3,188 feet) was one of those which has impressed upon me how pleasant it is to walk yourself thoroughly dry after being as thoroughly wet. The mountain, which is one of the tops of Ben Eighe, stands boldly south-west of Kinlochewe; the epithet "Ban" referring to the light-coloured rock around the summit.

I was staying at Strathpeffer that August, and one morning took the train as far as Achnasheen, then a 'bus to Kinlochewe. The weather was enigmatic; the "hunch" that often serves me in familiar localities told me nothing of the meaning of the sky. It was a uniform grey, but the hills were clear to the tops. Some local fellow-passengers assured me it would be fine; that, I suppose, was out of Highland politeness.

I have seldom known a wetter day than it made up its mind to be soon after a 'bus deposited me at Kinlochewe. One of the old inhabitants of that place warned me that my mountain was "a deil to master," and recommended me to approach it up the glen that runs conspicuously down cleaving the eastern flank. I did not take his advice, but made for the open to the south of the glen, which I knew would be soaking underfoot in the driest of weather, and I can certify that Sgurr Ban is not a deil to master. A good rough scramble, I should call it.

What I saw of the hill and its surroundings was, I must admit, very little; my view was restricted to a

circle of a few yards diameter. I scrambled enclosed
in drenching cloud, but reached the summit all right.
A ridge that looked most interesting ran northwards
from the top—interesting, narrow and wild. Wondering if I might make a descent in that direction, I
explored it for a short distance, but was presently
aware of an obstacle that, looming through the cloud,
wore an exceedingly forbidding appearance. It was
a pinnacle on the top of my ridge—one of the three,
known as the Black Regiment, which you can see from
the valley.

I learned afterwards that those pinnacles are not
as bad as they look ; they certainly could not be as
formidable as that half-seen menace suggested. My
informant was an expert rock-climber, however, and I
suggest that the " average hill-walker " would do as I
did, and decide not to attempt to traverse them.

The descent of Sgurr Ban, as regards the upper
portion, was rather more trying than the ascent. That
white cape the mountain wears so conspicuously
consists of loose chunks of quartz, making a kind of
big scree on which to sprain an ankle would be easier
than in avoiding a slip. Put your weight on one chunk,
and all those around start to shift, but not with the
flowing motion of some types of smaller scree, on and
with which you can comfortably slide. It does not cover
any great extent, but till you are off it, every step is a
matter for a little care. As I descended parts of that
hill-face, the rattle of the moving scree was like the
noise of a stone-breaker at work, and another odd
sound-effect of that day was the deep roar of a stream
somewhere below me in the cloud.

In that wet windy thickness I headed a good deal

too far south, and had a mile or two to tramp before getting back to Kinlochewe. I was rewarded, however, by some of those strange and beautiful effects seen amongst the mountains when a bad day begins to change its mood, as this was doing. Great shadowy mountain-shapes began to loom here and there, some seeming suspended above the grey vapour. More and more clearly they emerged ; the rain stopped, and now I had a hunch all right ; the evening would be sunny.

Refreshing myself with hot tea and some food at Kinlochewe, I realised just how wet I was by the uselessnesss of my fingers to handle anything ; it seemed as if the rain had for once got through my skin—no towelling was able to make them feel dry. How enjoyable was the trudge back up Glendochart I cannot explain. Every minute the mist grew brighter ; ever and anon colour and sparkle spread around as the sun really came through for a moment, and those genial appearances grew longer and more frequent, until presently they were no more obscured, and I walked on, with the evening warmth full on my back, and my clothes drying rapidly as I went. The condition of the map—a new one—which I used that day—is a permanent reminder of the general " humidity " of that outing.

I was never more luxuriously comfortable than when I reached Achnasheen again, passenger for the last mile or two on a lorry carrying oildrums. On the road in Glen Dochartie, by the way, I found a curious thing—a roll of cloth, which, opened, revealed that it was a container of needles. Hundreds of them were there, from huge to tiny ones—perhaps a pedlar's stock-in-trade. Unfortunately rust had got at them, and I rolled the thing up and left it. Perhaps some Highland housewife found it, and, after the application of oil and perseverance, supplied herself and her neighbours with a life-time's needle-store.

CHAPTER THIRTY-TWO

BEN WYVIS

THE Ben Wyvis group looks so fine as a background to many a view from the south that if you are anywhere near Inverness and love the highest when you see it, it is an irresistible magnet. I was staying at Strathpeffer when I paid my one and only visit, and I have reason to think, from what intimates of the mountain have said to me, that my hasty impressions do not do it justice.

Strathpeffer is unlike any Scottish village I know; in its sheltered position, and with all its trees and gardens, it always makes me think of a carefully arranged basket of flowers. North-east of it, really on the first slopes of Wyvis, is a group of hamlets which I found fascinating—Bottacks, Heights of Flodderty, Heights of Brae, and the rest. I like the way they snuggle along the slopes, and their stone dykes and meandering paths. My approach was from Achterneed, and the map indicated a path for the first mile or two. It wasn't obvious to me, so I didn't waste time hunting for it, but made straight up the soft, rough braes towards the gap between Little Wyvis and An Cabar (3,106 feet), which is the southerly top of the group which is covered by the name Wyvis.

I found it rather laborious going, without any particular interest, but the surroundings beautiful with mosses of the most brilliant colours; the month was August, a good one for those decorations.

The prospect from that summit must be grand on a

THE APPROACH TO BEN WYVIS

W.K.H.

really clear day ; for me it was hazy, with clouds hanging around the high tops.

The top of Ben Wyvis is unique in my experience, with its deep soft moss ; under my boots it felt like a rich-piled carpet, while on most hills of anything like that elevation the moss clings close to the rock, and in summer is dry and harsh to the tread. It occurred to me that both the surface and the formation would have allowed a horseman to gallop all the way—perhaps a couple of miles—from An Cabar to Glas Leathad Mor (3,429 feet), the highest point, the real top of Wyvis. It didn't seem anything like that height, and I remember saying on my return that Wyvis was just an elevated moor—to be reproached by a friend who assured me that a little exploration would have shown me that Wyvis was not all so tame.

Well, it was not a day to wander further, even had time been at my disposal. I had only just reached the cairn on the summit when wisps of mist began to blow around it, suggesting that unless I wanted a different sort of expedition from the easy one I had prepared for, I had better be getting to lower levels. So I put on a little speed and made towards Bottacks. Good sort of country, I found, for a descent. Amongst the wild life I noticed ptarmigan and golden plover, and more white hares than I had ever seen on a hill. Coming over a little ridge I scattered a group of about a dozen—and began to understand the astonishing winter bags of Ben Wyvis white hares of which I had read. Doubtless that luxuriant growth of moss, characteristic of these hills, accounts for the numbers of these hardy little mountaineers.

Most vivid amongst my recollections of that

afternoon, however, is the behaviour of the mist. I
was familiar enough with mist on hills, but the swiftness
with which it gathered that day on the summits and
the pace at which it seemed to roll down in pursuit of
me, thick, not a mere vapoury cloud-wreath, were
eye-openers. Perhaps Wyvis is noted for the quick
gathering of such mists, but I indulged the fancy, as I
retreated, that the mountain had a mind to show me
that I had taken it altogether too lightly. I found
the path this time, and an exceedingly attractive one
it is, winding amongst boulders through deep heather.

CHAPTER THIRTY-THREE

SGOR THUILM AND THE CORRIE OF THE BIRCHES

IT would surprise me if many readers could at once place Sgor Thuilm on the map, though it is one of the noble company of hills above three thousand feet in height, being actually 3,164 feet. Definitely it is off the beaten track, and no special distinction can perhaps be claimed for it. Amongst my recollections, however, it figures as the pretext for one of the grandest tramps I have ever had in the Highlands. Every circumstance contributed to make it so, including the weather and the company.

Our expedition took place in May, one year when that month had the still and brilliant warmth that we fondly expect from July. So hot and windless it was that returning from Morar when the week-end was over, I saw the deer standing on the tops of knolls quite near, disregarding the noisy smoky monster rushing past, for the sake of some breath of cooler air.

On the morning fixed for our tramp over Sgor Thuilm I left Fort William by an early train, and found my two friends awaiting me at Glenfinnan station. Both were soldiers on leave, and both belonged to a unit famed for its physical fitness, so I knew I had to be on my toes.

Not taking time even to have a near look at the Prince Charlie monument standing at the head of the Loch, there quite close to the station, we set off up Glenfinnan—and I still seem to be sensible of the

strength of the morning sun on my back. I will not
spend words on describing the glen, or even the climb
to our selected summit ; anywhere in the Highlands
in May, and in such weather, is as nearly perfect, surely,
as anything terrestrial can be. The heat was
oppressive, I suppose, till we got above two thousand
feet ; beyond that the sun never seems too hot, and the
air, diamond clear, almost always has a bracing quality.

Drifts still lay in crannies and other sheltered
spots. All day we saw no other human beings. The
sheep we encountered suggested by their shyness that
our species was a rarity in the neighbourhood ; deer
and ptarmigan were commoner. (And what a picture
of wild nature was shown to us for an instant as a
hind shied in her easy canter when a ptarmigan got up
close to her feet!). It was surprising, to me at least,
to raise a heron right amongst the tops. It was the only
time I have seen one so high.

Our aim was to cross the mountain and such
ridges and switchbacks as presented themselves, to
descend into Glen Plean, walk down it to the head of
Loch Morar, and then, by a track indicated on the
northern side, to make for Morar, expecting to reach
a hospitable house there by perhaps half-past seven.

Our estimate of the time required was almost
exactly five hours short, and the extension certainly
was not due to lingering by the way.

For one thing, the hill-tops were a good deal more
rugged than we had anticipated ; for another, the
drop into Glen Plean was very much steeper. Perhaps
I should be justified in saying it was precipitous, and
we were glad of handholds offered by the countless
little birch-trees clinging to the rock. Birches, those

ON SGURR THUILM, GLENFINNAN

W.K.H.

lovely trees, were characteristic of the surprising gorge in which, after our scramble down, we found ourselves —and was not this named on the map Coire a Bheithe, the Corrie of the Birches ? We had descended about the top of the Corrie, which is rather a glen running west to the head of Loch Morar. At the eastern side of the watershed starts the real Glen Plean, with its tiny lochan Leum an t-Sagairt, "the loch of the Priest's Leap," whence runs the river Plean to empty itself into Loch Arkaig. The precipitous hillsides above the head of Glen Plean are remarkable for rock-masses rounded and smoothed by glacial action—typical examples of what the geologist calls *roches moutonnées*.

Well, we had scrambled down into that profound cleft, not without caution and many detours, thinking that its attainment would mean that the day's rough stuff was over, and that all we had before us was a longish tramp into Morar. One look round was enough to demonstrate that we should have to think again. I doubt if I have ever been in a wilder-looking place. The glen or pass is quite narrow ; to right and left soar hill-sides everywhere almost precipitous, and here and there consisting of smooth perpendicular slabs. From these heights rocks of all sizes have fallen into the gorge. At its narrowest point it is almost blocked by one mass certainly larger than some modern houses. Inevitably into my mind came Scott's words as a suitable description—"rude fragments of an earlier world." The older masses were clothed with thick, close-growing moss ; between them yawned crevices and chasms, and all around, on the sides of this savagely beautiful mountain cleft and amongst the strewn debris with which it was half choked, flourished the fairy beauty of the birches, then in their new tender emerald foliage.

As for the track indicated by the map—all we could find to suggest that a human being had ever passed that way before was an occasional indication on one of the rare patches of turf, a scratch on one of the jumbled rocks. To me it would not have been surprising to catch a glimpse of a wolf, or some other supposedly-extinct wild animal, in that wild and fascinating place. What did meet us was more beautiful than a wolf—an owl, unexpectedly a-wing at that time of day. Perhaps my friends ahead had disturbed his noon siesta, so that I had the benefit. A big bird came towards me, flying almost noiselessly ; it was a tawny owl, and its round face with great solemn eyes was within a few yards of me before it banked and swerved away, wonderfully displaying the soft pale colours of its underwings with the sunlight shining through. A fitting tenant for the Corrie of the Birches.

The gorge seemed endless, to men now in a hurry. In the heat that constant scrambling, balancing and jumping amongst the rocks would have been wearisome had not the spell of the place and its untamed beauty kept us interested and astonished.

We emerged at last to the tranquil water's edge at the head of the Loch, and sought the path along the northern slopes. Again we felt a grievance against the cartographer. Either we never found the track indicated, or his ideas of paths are akin to those of the mountain goat. Here again there was little sign of " traffic," but questionable marks, few and far between ; and the rocky, heathery slope is so abrupt that the dark water seemed almost straight below us.

We were tired by this time, and hungry, but we made our forced march through the hours of an evening of the most heavenly beauty. The gloaming was luminous with the sunset's afterglow, and with that after-glow presently merged the golden light of a full moon. The surface of the loch a hundred or two feet below us reflected all the soft colours of the tranquil sky, and held another golden moon ; and from the other side a belated cuckoo called time after time ; and —the man in front of me was seized with an attack of hiccoughs, as persistent as the bird. The moon, the serene sky, the cuckoo, and that hiccough, are all revived in my memory every time I see or hear the name of Loch Morar.

There really is a road into Morar from Tarbet, about half-way down the loch.

The walk, as we did it, I do not recommend to any but those in particularly good form ; it calls for a considerable amount of stamina, and is not one of those expeditions which can be curtailed by some short cut from half way.

The easiest way to visit the Corrie of the Birches would be to sail to the head of Loch Morar and then walk into the gorge as far as you fancied. There is a cottage called Oban at the head of the Loch, a fact worth remembering if it is inhabited when you plan your exploration.

Perhaps it is worth mentioning that we all three spent the following morning—another perfect one of blue and gold, a real Morar morning—paddling with some youngsters in the warm shallows over the white sand. It was the ideal sequel, from every point of view, to such a day as the one we had spent on the hills.